This is a fabulous book, smart, detailed and right on the money to help any small business work with any big business. Great work Bronwyn Reid.

Small businesses have been struggling for decades to crack the code of working with big business. Bronwyn Reid has written a book based on many years of experience, offering both practical and inspirational advice that will help any small business to attract bigger customers, keep working with them for longer periods of time and ensure that the relationship is mutually profitable and rewarding. It's about time someone wrote such an intelligent and useful book for the small business market.

—*Andrew Griffiths, International Bestselling Author*

For small business wanting to crack a big corporate contract, Bronwyn Reid shares her years of experience in an easy to read format, the risks, the benefits and the whole process from whoa to go (or not).

—*Amanda Fisher, The Numbers Matter, Author of Unscramble Your Numbers, The Connected Accounting Practice, Connected Technology.*

Bronwyn develops sincere and genuine relationships with stakeholders and like-minded people striving to achieve similar organisational and community change. Some people are driven to networking as job requirements and KPIs or as a means to increase the bottom line of their company budget; I can state that Bronwyn doesn't fit this mould – she engages and networks with people because she wants to make a difference and to share her learning from experience with others, so that they perhaps don't make some of the same mistakes that she and Ian did when first starting out in small business some twenty odd years ago.

Small Company, Big Business explains how to work with Government, Private Enterprise, 'the Big End of Town' companies, legal requires, systems – technology or not, project management and finances – a must read for all SME owners wanting to work in the Big Business arena.

—*Kim Harrington, Associate Vice-Chancellor Rockhampton Region, and, Director of Business Development CQUniversity Australia*

INDEPENDENT

First published 2017 by Bronwyn Reid
This revised edition published 2023
PO Box 1638, Carindale
Queensland 4152 Australia

Copyright © Bronwyn Reid 2017

All rights reserved. Except as permitted under the *Australian Copyright Act 1968*, no part of this publication may be reproduced, stored in a retrieval system, or transmitted in any form or by any means, electronic, mechanical, photocopying, recording or otherwise, without prior written permission from the publisher. All enquiries should be made to the author.

Cover design by BrandStrong
Edited by Anne-Maree Tripp
Illustrations by CADesignIT
Typeset in 12/16.5 pt Adobe Garamond Pro by Post Pre-press Group, Brisbane

Cataloguing-in-Publication data is available from the
National Library of Australia

ISBN 978-0-6451277-5-1 (pbk)
ISBN 978-0-6451277-6-8 (epub)
ISBN 978-0-6451277-7-5 (kindle)

Disclaimer:
Any information in the book is purely the opinion of the author based on her personal experience and should not be taken as business or legal advice. All material is provided for educational purposes only. We recommend to always seek the advice of a qualified professional before making any decision regarding personal and business needs.

SMALL COMPANY BIG BUSINESS

How to Find, Win and Keep Big Customers

BRONWYN REID

CONTENTS

Preface to The Second Edition — ix
Introduction — 1

SECTION 1: HOW DO BIG BUYERS THINK? — 7

Chapter 1   Three Disconnects — 9
Chapter 2   How Do Big Buyers Buy? — 13
Chapter 3   What's A Supply Chain and How Do They Work? — 16
Chapter 4   What Do Large Buyers Want? — 23
Chapter 5   Why Would They Buy from Me? — 26
Chapter 6   What Would Prevent Them Buying from Me? — 37
Chapter 7   Understanding Contracts — 51

SECTION 2: SHOULD I PRESS THE GO BUTTON ... OR NOT? — 73

Chapter 8   Do You REALLY Want to Supply to Big Organisations? — 75
Chapter 9   The Business Journey — 79
Chapter 10 The Rewards to Be Enjoyed — 86
Chapter 11 Reasons Not to Do This — 89

SECTION 3: SET YOUR FOUNDATIONS — 93

Chapter 12 The Nine Essential Business Skills — 95

Chapter 13	What Business Are You In?	98
Chapter 14	What's Your Purpose?	101
Chapter 15	What's in Your PESTLE Environment?	105
Chapter 16	Who Is Your Ideal Customer?	107
Chapter 17	You Have to Pay the Admission Price	111
Chapter 18	Understanding Portfolio Risk—Having All Your Eggs in One Basket	113
Chapter 19	Your External Team	118
Chapter 20	Financial Management—Getting Paid	127
Chapter 21	Growth, Downsizing, and Exit Strategies	134

SECTION 4: SIMPLIFY THE COMPLEXITY — 137

Chapter 22	Why Your Business Needs Systems	139
Chapter 23	The Business Benefits of Good Systems—the 5 Cs	147
Chapter 24	The Seven Steps to Creating Systems	154
Chapter 25	The Technology Question	173
Chapter 26	Do I Need to be Certified?	177

SECTION 5: MAKE YOURSELF KNOWN — 187

Chapter 27	To Be or Not to Be—Online	189
Chapter 28	Your Email Is a Big Part of Your Brand	191
Chapter 29	Your Website	195
Chapter 30	Getting Behind the Barriers	199
Chapter 31	Partnerships	206

SECTION 6: TELL YOUR STORY — 217

Chapter 32	The Importance of Storytelling	219
Chapter 33	Capability Statements	223
Chapter 34	Bids, Tenders, Proposals—What?	227

Chapter 35	Tenders and Proposals—How They Work and Where to Find Them	235
Chapter 36	Start Local	239
Chapter 37	Go/No-Go Decisions	242
Chapter 38	Writing Tenders and Proposals	245

SECTION 7: SO YOU'VE WON THE CONTRACT—NOW WHAT? 255

Chapter 39	Introduction to Project Management	257
Chapter 40	Keep Your Customer Close	269
Chapter 41	Putting it All Together	273

| Further Information and Resources | 281 |
| Ordering Additional Copies of this Book | 285 |

PREFACE TO THE SECOND EDITION

Covid-19 confirmed many of the principles and pieces of advice that were contained in the first edition of this book which was released in 2017. Critical things such as:
- Being prepared for a crisis, or even a business exit
- The supreme importance of risk in supply chains
- Making sure that the contracts you use, or are subject to, are fit for purpose
- Having a good relationship with your financier in case you need their help
- Being hyper-aware of what is happening around you in the business environment (your PESTLE analysis)
- Paying attention to your online digital presence, and by extension, being able to conduct business online.

But what's really different since then and why did I feel the need to update this book as a result?

Covid changed us all. The Covid-19 pandemic has brought about significant changes that cannot be ignored.

We know that every downturn has an upturn. What also holds

true is that every major downturn brings a technology change that has far-reaching effects. If we look at busts throughout history, and then look a decade ahead, you will always find some of the biggest companies and brands emerged from the debris. There are always companies that look around, work out that the landscape has changed, and then create products and services that suit the new environment. Often, the new technology will take a long time to emerge, and even longer to become all-pervading and a common part of our lives. Typically, only about 3% of people are early adopters who lead the way. Meanwhile, laggards may take another 5–10 years to catch up, and in about 30 years, none of us can imagine living life without the new invention.

Unfortunately, those who lag behind may be left behind. A recent example is the aftermath of the dot-com bust in 2000. The kings of the current stock market – the technology companies such as Facebook, Amazon and Alphabet (Google) – all emerged out of that upheaval.

Along with Apple and Microsoft, these companies currently make up 50 percent of the US Technology Stock Market Index (the Nasdaq), and one-fifth of the main US Stock Index, the S&P 500. They didn't even exist 30 years ago.

Now, as a group, the tech titans Amazon, Apple, Facebook and Google are coming under increasing scrutiny over their operating methods, transparency and corporate ethics. (Incidentally, as of November 2020, the "tech barons" had accumulated an additional $565 billion in wealth since the COVID-19 pandemic started.)

Who knows what the disruptive technology emerging from the 2020 downturn will be? Something to do with climate change? Artificial intelligence? Quantum computing? Or something that we haven't even heard of yet? We will have to wait and see, but there is another question to be answered as well.

Note that I included Artificial Intelligence in my list of possible disruptive technologies above. On November 30, 2022, ChatGPT landed, at this point in time there were already a host of entrants in this emerging field but ChatGPT stepped up the AI race to a frenzied pace. As of May 2023, when this book is heading off to the printer, AI is looking to be an odds-on bet as the disruptive technology that will define the next era.

While this concept has been discussed in academic circles and the "fringe press" for some time, it's now making headlines in mainstream media. Some companies have already embraced this change, but others are slow to catch on.

New technology is emerging that could displace or at the very least disrupt the current technology titans, those same companies that dominate the stock market, what are the implications for stock market values, and therefore us? All we can be sure of is that some disruption will emerge, and it will dramatically change the way we do business.

INTRODUCTION

Being a small business owner is a bit like being on a perpetual roller-coaster ride. There are the adrenaline highs (remember that moment when you got your Business Registration Certificate in the post that you could frame and put on the office wall?), and deep, despairing lows (like the day your best customer called up and informed you they were taking their entire contract to your competitor). Your bank account is constantly in a state of either feast or famine. There are sleepless nights when you just have to keep working to meet a client deadline. And then there is the never-ending search for new leads and new customers.

There is also the consistency of the dream that one day you will finally land a really big and highly profitable company as a client. Instead of constantly chasing leads and having a wildly fluctuating bank account, your new contract will provide you with a steady and certain income. You also know just how much it will mean to your business to be able to put the logo of your new customer on your website and marketing materials—especially if it is a well-known brand—proudly proclaiming that you are one of their trusted suppliers. You can do what you've always done, just on a bigger scale.

Since 2020 and the global Covid-19 pandemic, we've become used to the phrase "it's all different now". While doing big business with high-paying large companies might have once been a simple goal, the issues of supply chain challenges have made it even harder to navigate this territory in recent times. Because supply chain challenges have made it both easier and harder for SMEs to do *big business* as a *small company*.

As enticing as the idea of doing "big business" may be, most small business owners simply don't know how or where to start to make this a reality. They don't understand what big customers **want**, and they don't understand their **language**. In fact, seven out of ten small business owners tell me that this is their biggest obstacle to growing their business by attracting a big customer. Six out of ten say that they don't know how to get their potential big customers to even notice them.

That was me 26 years ago. Our consultancy business had the opportunity to sign a contract with an international research organisation, but I really didn't know where to start. I felt powerless. It was me—or at least my husband and me—trying to figure out how to deal with an international giant. And the deal we came away with reflected that imbalance of knowledge. I simply didn't have the knowledge or the tools to do any better at the time, but I knew instinctively that we'd had the bad end of the deal. I knew that if our fledgling business had any chance of a long-term future, I had to get better at dealing with these people.

The same feelings of confusion, trepidation, and lack of knowledge may be stopping you from taking that one important leap you need to get your business really growing—stepping up and becoming a supplier to a big organisation. You may have heard horror stories about not getting paid, 90–120 day payment terms, or overwhelming and pedantic bureaucracy. But it doesn't have to be all gloom and doom.

Fast forward 26 years, and I have certainly done a lot of learning. Our consultancy company went on to become an award-winning, successful supplier to all levels of government, and national and international private and public companies. I stumbled along and tried a countless number of ways to make the interaction with my big customers smoother. The lessons I learned and the mistakes I made along the way have enabled me to now help other small business owners grow their own businesses into the vehicle they envisaged when they started out, back when all they really had was a certificate of incorporation and a dream.

I have distilled all those lessons—some painful and expensive—into a program that others can follow to make their own path easier. That's what this book is about. I've put it all into a logical sequence so you can implement gradually, rather than feeling completely overwhelmed. If you are reading this book, you are most probably already thinking about trying to get those important big customers. You have probably even attended some workshops to learn what to do. Chances are, though, that the implementation—putting it all into place—is still looking like an impossible jungle.

That is where my expertise lies.

Since departing the corporate life and setting up our first small business, I have dealt with international agribusiness companies, NGOs, every level of government, large corporations and supermarkets, and resources companies ranging in size from "juniors" to the global corporate giants like BHP Billiton and Rio Tinto. Much of the work I have done over the past 15 years has been with the Australian mining and oil and gas sectors, so many of my anecdotes and case studies in this book relate to that industry. However, please don't think that the principles and methods I write about in this book are applicable only to the resources industry. Yes, the mining and oil and gas industries are particularly fastidious, but the principles are equally applicable to any large buyer. And believe me, if you can jump the high bar set by these companies, you will be ready to deal with any big buyer, anywhere.

A Simple Seven-Step Framework

The seven steps outlined in this book will allow you to find, engage, and then keep those big customers you really, *really* want to have featured on your website as clients you work with. You will learn how they think, what they expect of you, what you need in order to comply with their requirements, and how to keep them on your client list once you have signed that first important contract.

It is important that all seven steps of the framework be implemented. Your new, big customers set a high bar, and expect it to be maintained. It's the same as building a house. **You can't build a solid house on wobbly foundations, and you can't build a sustainable business without doing the preparatory work.** However, once you have invested the time and money to transform your business into one that has the qualifications and capabilities to be a trusted supplier to large organisations, working with any customer of any size will be a whole lot easier and more profitable.

As I mentioned earlier, I have made my fair share of mistakes over the years and this book is the result of what I've learned. I hope that it will be of use to you, and that it will shorten your path to working successfully with big business.

A Quick Explanation of Some Jargon And Clarity Around Size

If school economics was decades ago for you or you stumbled into being an entrepreneur without having been enlightened to these descriptions, don't worry, you're not alone. Many of us wonder what actually constitutes being a *small* business versus a *big* business.

This book refers to small, medium and big (or large) business, so let's first define what we mean when we use those terms. I wish the definitions were straightforward but, unfortunately, they are not—far from it.

We use the terms "small business" and "SME" (small and medium sized enterprises) rather loosely—perhaps with good reason. If we think of a continuum with my environmental consultancy at one end, and Rio Tinto (one of our clients) at the other end, there's not much argument to be had. My company is clearly a small business, and Rio Tinto is obviously a large business. (For those who don't know, Rio Tinto is a major multinational resources company with revenue of $40 billion.)

But in between those two extremes, there is room for a lot of interpretation—and everyone has a different interpretation. Here are just a few examples of different definitions of "small business" used within Australia:

- **Australian Taxation Office (ATO):** A company with an annual revenue of less than $10 million (excluding GST).
- **Australian Government:** Who knows? Different legislation uses different benchmarks, so it could be $2 million, $10 million, $25 million or $50 million—or any other number that they think will be electorally palatable.
- **Australian Securities and Exchange Commission (ASIC):** A company with two out of three of the following: an annual revenue of less than $50 million, fewer than 100 employees and gross assets of less than $25 million.
- **Fair Work Australia:** A company with fewer than 15 employees.
- **Australian Bureau of Statistics:** A company with fewer than 20 employees.
- **Queensland State Government:** A company with fewer than 20 employees.
- **BHP Local Buying Program:** A company with annual revenue of less than $10 million.
- **Australian Competition and Consumer Commission (ACCC):** A company with fewer than 20 employees, including casuals.

The definitions get even more diverse when we look overseas. In the USA, the Small Business Administration sets either annual revenue or employee count limits for different industry sectors[1]. In the UK, a small business has fewer than 50 employees, annual revenue of less than £10.2 million and a balance sheet worth of less than £5.1 million.

Our Definition

For the purposes of this book, I'm going to stick with the following guidelines: a ***small business*** is one that has 20 employees or less, a ***medium business*** is one that has between 20 and 200 employees, and a ***big (or large) business*** is one that has more than 200 employees.

I prefer not to cloud the issue with turnover figures as they can vary so much—to the point where the definitions become nonsensical. After all, I'm sure you will agree that a company employing 100 people with an annual turnover of only, say, $300,000 is another way of saying "no money at all".

---

[1] https://www.sba.gov/document/support-table-size-standards

SECTION 1
HOW DO BIG BUYERS THINK?

Almost every small business owner starts their business venture with the hope of eventually landing a big-name company as a client. Instead of constantly chasing leads and having a bank account balance that looks like the initial design for a roller coaster, your new contract will provide you with a steady and certain income. But before you start chasing this particular rainbow, it is extremely important to understand that big companies are different. If you are used to dealing with other small or medium businesses, you will have to adjust to a whole new way of doing business. Understanding this at the outset will save you a lot of time, angst, and probably money.

Section 1 of this book will give you an insight into the big buyer's brain. Delve in, have a look around, and get an idea of how your "big buyer" thinks and operates.

Chapter 1
Three Disconnects

During my more than 25 years of creating and running businesses, I've talked and worked with hundreds of other business owners who, like me, were trying to work successfully with big buyers. Whether the buyer in question was a big company, something to do with government, a state-owned enterprise or whatever, I kept seeing the same problems come up time and time again. Then, when I started to build Small Company, Big Business, I interviewed and surveyed many small business owners to try and find out the problems and hurdles they had when trying to win contracts with these sorts of buyers. Again, the same themes emerged, and I found that I could group them all into three categories.

1. **Complexity.** Big companies and government have a whole raft of "prerequisites" that must be put in place before they will deal with you, and these can change all the time. Sometimes they seem to not even know what they want themselves. In this confusing environment, it is very hard for the small business owner to figure out exactly what is required of them.
2. **Cost and time.** Implementing all the prerequisites and making the necessary changes to your business is a time-consuming and

costly exercise. And then you have to keep everything up to date. All this requires a considerable amount of money, time, and energy. For some, it's all just too much and they walk away. For those who accept the challenge, putting it all in place can take years, and a lot of time and money can be wasted trying different solutions.

3. **Getting "on the radar".** Most small businesses struggle to get "on the radar" of large corporations, and get a foot in the door. In fact, from my own research, some 70% of business owners say this is their number one hurdle in winning contracts with large buyers, who seem to exist behind an impenetrable iron curtain.

When I made the decision to write this book, I began to look for research that was already out there, and what had already been written about how small businesses could successfully become suppliers to big organisations. What I very quickly found was that there was a considerable amount of research on the topic, ***but it was almost exclusively written from the big business' point of view.*** There is a wide variety of literature—everything from short blog posts to scholarly academic articles to entire books—on how big companies can successfully engage with small companies. Much of it is written with the background of how the bigger company can fulfil its corporate social responsibility (CSR) or local content obligations.

What I found interesting though, was that the same three themes emerged again—only this time from the big business' (or government) point of view. From this point of view, their problems are:

1. **Small companies just don't understand how supply chains work.** They don't understand the concept of risk, and why big companies "vet" their suppliers thoroughly before committing to buy from them.

2. **Small businesses don't have good enough systems** that will allow them to reliably deliver a consistent, quality product.
3. **Big businesses and government have strict procurement procedures and protocols**, and can be restricted in who and what kind of businesses they can purchase from. Often, they will grant just a few large contracts to a few large suppliers, and allow them to take on the task of recruiting smaller, specialist suppliers.

After much thought, I eventually captured all this in my *Three Disconnects* diagram.

Trying to bridge the disconnect gap between the two parties became the purpose of the Small Company, Big Business program. The program has changed and evolved since my first research was conducted, but the basic premise of two parties looking at the same problem in different ways remains.

As a result of these disconnects, B2B (business-to-business) commerce is too often limited to big business-to-big business. That is what I want to challenge by writing this book.

Chapter 2
How Do Big Buyers Buy?

Our consultancy company was started when we returned to Australia after several years of wandering the planet. My husband's work in plantation agriculture had given us some amazing life experiences in some wonderful places. However, when our first child was born, we felt it was time to head home to Australia.

Ian and his colleague Thomas were offered the opportunity to write a series of technical manuals on plantation agriculture, bringing together all their experience and successes implementing best management practices. The publishing was to be funded by an international agricultural research organisation, and they offered a contract which, while it was a significant amount of money, contained some aspects that we weren't happy with. However, the cost of publishing was way beyond our means. The books were to be printed on thick, coated paper with a strong spiral binding so they could be used in-field easily and without damage. This was before the days of easy self-publishing.

In the end, the deal offered was on a one-off, upfront, "take it or leave it" basis. We took it, and that was our very first contract. It did give our fledgling company a giant boost, but we knew that we had foregone a significant amount of money. And so it proved to be. Over the ensuing years, the books sold some 30,000 copies. That was our first experience of trying to negotiate with an international organisation and we realised just how unprepared we were.

Some five years later, we had the opportunity to tender for a multi-million dollar research contract in the agricultural industry that encompassed two levels of government as well as private industry—from the federal government right down to individual farmers. This was my introduction to dealing with government contracts, and I had to go on a very rapid and steep learning curve. This included working out how to deal with this beast called government bureaucracy and its seemingly incessant reporting requirements. In fact, we almost pulled out of the contracts before they even started. I discovered that governments work so slowly that sometimes you really have to wonder how they get anything done at all. We had all the resources in place for the projects to begin, but the release of the funding to actually start doing anything had ground to a halt somewhere in a government office. I was at the point of dismissing staff and selling equipment when finally the first tranche of funds was released.

This led to an opportunity to start dealing with the resources industry—coal mining companies to be specific, and later oil and gas companies. At that time, the enormous resources industry boom brought on by the rapid industrialisation of China was just getting started. We tendered for, and won, our first small ($40,000) contract with a mining giant. I thought dealing with government was time consuming, but nothing had prepared me for dealing with resources companies. Like government, large resources companies are huge, lumbering giants, controlled by procedures. I felt as though I was constantly stumbling around in the dark, trying to comply with everything that was asked of us—another form to fill out, another qualification to complete, another "thing" to do. Every time I thought I understood, a new requirement popped up to be dealt with.

In fact this was not my first experience of being a small supplier to very large organisations. I had the great fortune to grow up as a "farm kid" in regional Queensland. My family's agribusiness operations were negotiating with and supplying to Australia's large supermarket chains, and from this I learned that ruthless efficiency is also part of the mix when dealing with big businesses. Produce can be rejected on the slightest pretext, and contracts summarily terminated. **A recent addition to the large retailer's practices is to not pay the supplier until the produce is sold through the checkout.**

As a result of all these early experiences, I came to realise that regardless of their industry, big buyers are different, and your key to success as a supplier is to understand this. Treating your big company customers in the same manner as your existing clients simply won't do. Instead of being a single supplier to a single customer, **you become a link in their corporate supply chain**.

Chapter 3
What's A Supply Chain and How Do They Work?

By their very nature, large organisations have many suppliers—maybe hundreds of thousands of them. Each of those suppliers, including your small business, has their own suppliers, forming a ***supply chain***. Even if you are supplying directly to the big company, you are still considered to be a part of the supply chain.

The supply chain is a cascading series of transactions that end with the final consumer receiving the goods or services they required.

As with any chain, if one link breaks, the entire chain fails. The big company doesn't get their required products or services, so they can't supply their customers, who in turn become very, very unhappy.

Think of all the thousands of products that your local supermarket sells. They come from all sorts of suppliers and from thousands of different locations. Somehow, all that produce, all those packets and tins, end up on your local supermarket shelf. There is an entire network of companies, people, resources, and information involved in getting all those goods onto your supermarket shelf.

This network is the supermarket's supply chain.

The first step in understanding how big buyers buy is to understand the concept of a supply chain, and that you are just one, small link in that chain.

The best way to explain a supply chain is by using a diagram.

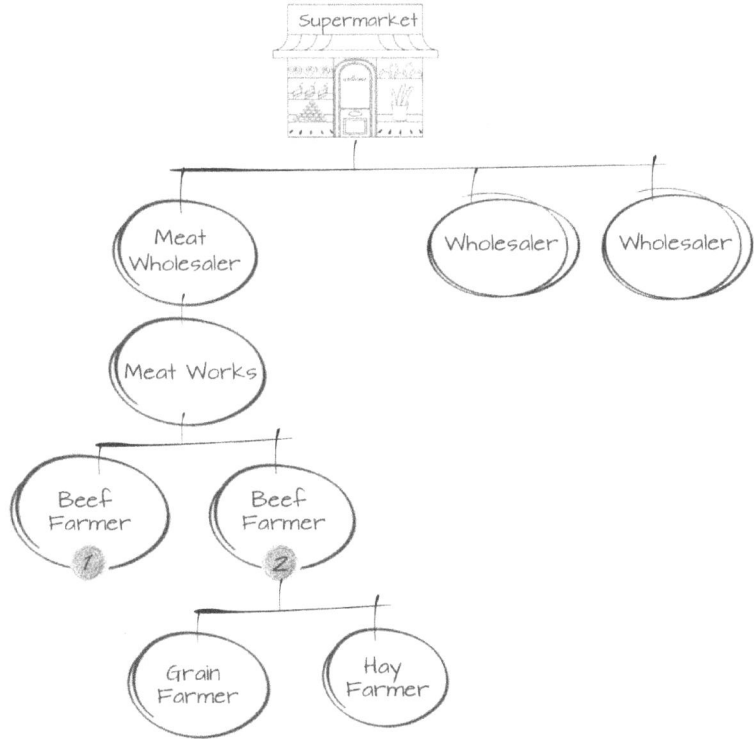

Tiers—Like a Wedding Cake

Supply chain and procurement people talk about *tiers*. The company selling directly to a large organisation is called a Tier 1 supplier. In our supply chain diagram, that is the meat wholesaler. The meatworks would be a Tier 2 supplier, the farmer a Tier 3 supplier, and so on.

You, as a small business owner, may fit in to the supply chain at any point, and you may already be in the chain as a Tier 4 or Tier 5 supplier. Our goal is to move up the supply chain, and secure Tier 2 and Tier 1 companies as our clients. That's where the credibility is, and where the sizeable contracts you need are sitting and waiting for you.

You can see quite quickly how the supermarket has more to be concerned about than just their immediate Tier 1 suppliers—like their meat wholesaler. Imagine there is a natural disaster and all the grain crops in an area are destroyed. All of a sudden, the farmer can't buy grain to feed her cattle, so she won't have any fat cattle ready to sell to the meatworks, who in turn won't have any steaks to sell to the meat wholesaler, which leads to you not being able to buy a steak for dinner. Or maybe the workers at the meatworkers all go on strike for higher pay. Same result—no steak for you for dinner. Covid-19 supply chain interruptions and recurring fires and flooding mean that more Australians now experience food insecurity.

As with most things, there are some large organisations that don't conform to the norm. Some of them use their own terminology for their supply chains, and you will find these out when you are doing your research on your target. Once you've figured that out, it's a very good idea to stick to using their words, not yours, as it demonstrates that you've taken the time to really find out about how they operate.

For one particular construction project, a small business was supplying at three different levels in the supply chain. It was supplying electronic measuring equipment directly to the construction company (Tier 1), to an engineering company contractor (Tier 2), and also to a company supplying to the same engineering contractor (Tier 3). Supply chains can get tangled sometimes.

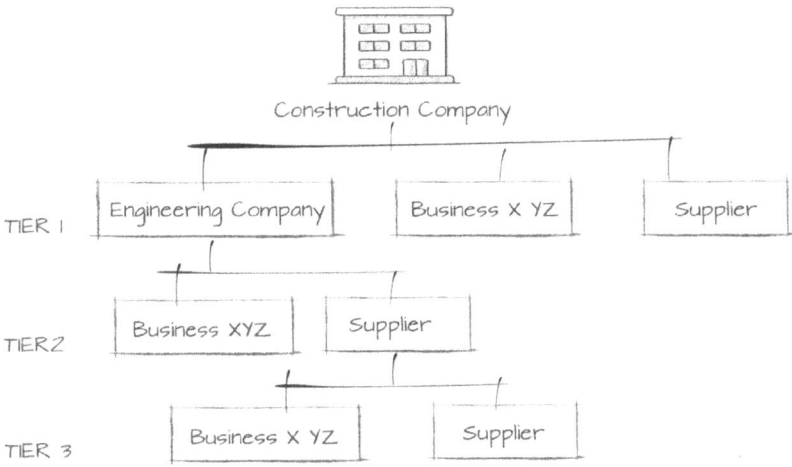

Supply chains can also get very long. Think about the T-shirt you may be wearing at the moment. The cotton may have been grown in Australia, then sent overseas for milling, then being sent to a Bangladeshi garment factory to be made into a T-shirt, and finally imported back to Australia for you to buy at a clothing store. The path from importer to store also includes a stop in Customs for an agent to clear the imported stock, warehousing, sorting, packaging, and finally delivery from, say, a Melbourne warehouse to 20 stores in three different states of Australia.

That's all quite complicated, and global supply chains like this are highly standardised and systemised. Consequently, it can seem like a whole lot of bureaucracy to manage and reams of forms to fill out. This is usually the first hitch for most small businesses. It all just seems to be too hard to manage.

As far as the paperwork goes, sometimes there are multiple forms and spreadsheets to be filled out (I have seen a spreadsheet with 630 lines of questions to be answered!). It seems they want to know every single intimate detail about you and your company right from the very start, and then they keep asking questions the entire time you are working with them.

While this seems endless and frustrating, the reason they do this is to attempt to limit risk.

As it happened, the real risk lay precisely within those complicated but systemised supply chains. We all experienced what happens when the Covid-19 pandemic laid waste to global shipping and air transport. Everything stopped moving, and all manner of goods and services we had come to expect as a normal or even essential part of our lives simply weren't available.

The Single Tier 1 Supplier Structure

While all large organisations will have many suppliers—even thousands of them—in their supply chain, some use a different structure. This is mostly where there are large, multi-million dollar construction projects involved—such as when a mining company builds a new mine or a construction company undertakes an entirely new development such as a shopping centre, hotel complex, or school.

In these situations, the company at the top will grant a contract to just one Tier 1 supplier. It then becomes the Tier 1 supplier's task to find and recruit all the suppliers for Tier 2, Tier 3, and so on down the supply chain. **The one Tier 1 contract is called an EPC (engineering, procurement and construction) or an EPCM (engineering, procurement and construction management) contract.** This model has the effect of removing the large company at the top (the "project proponent") from contact with the smaller companies in their supply chain, and unless the big company directs, their policies on local sourcing and local content may not filter down through the EPC/EPCM contractor.

Bundling

Another common practice by big companies—again particularly in the resources and construction industries where there are big projects being developed—is the ***bundling*** of contracts. Here, a number of smaller parcels of work are bundled together into a larger work package. For example, a bundle might include builders, plumbers, and electrical workers, and another separate bundle might be decorators, painters, and tiling experts.

From the big buyer's point of view, they now only have to deal with one supplier instead of multiple suppliers, saving on administrative overheads. The obvious downside for the small business owner is that while they may be experts in one component of the package and be able to do a superb job, they are prevented from winning the work because they cannot perform all the tasks. The best way to overcome this is to form partnerships with other companies, and we will talk more about how to best go about this in Chapter 31.

Where Do You Fit?

You now understand what a supply chain is and how it works. But before you go out stalking your potential big customer, **it's important to find out exactly where you could fit in the supply chain**. Are you capable of moving up to being a Tier 1 or Tier 2 supplier? Or are you going to be limited to the bottom tiers? Remember, the requirements and expectations of your performance increase as you move up the supply chain and become more important to the big customer.

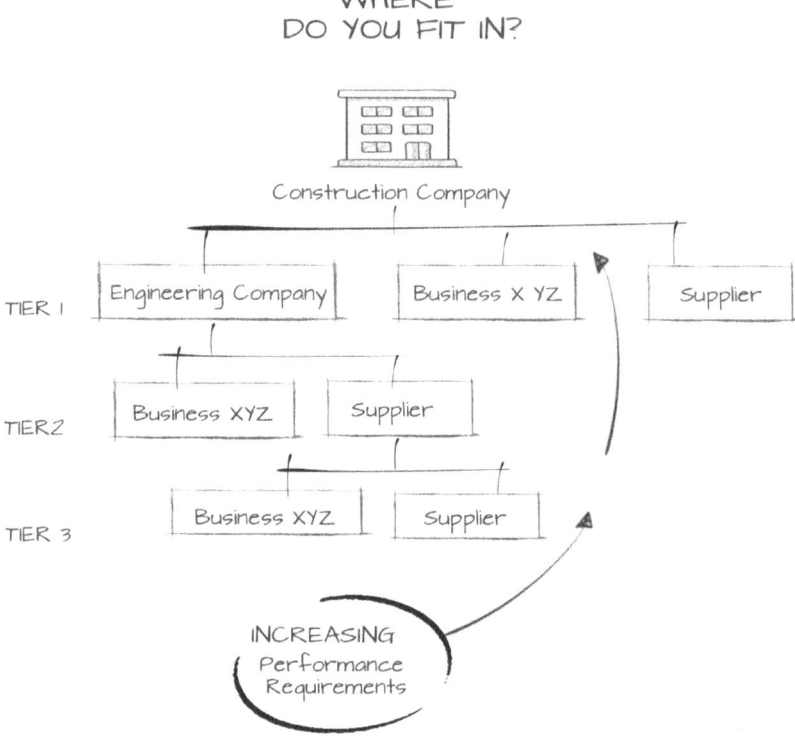

Included on the bronwynreid.com.au website is a short, 20-minute quiz that will give you some insight into where you may sit in a corporate supply chain, and where your business may need some attention.

Chapter 4
What Do Large Buyers Want?

This can be a very difficult question to answer because, very often, they don't actually know what they want themselves. I could recount any number of stories of contractors being given conflicting directions. What you can be sure of, however, is that any **confusion about requirements will be your fault**.

> *In the real world ...*
> *On one site, our personnel had been collecting water samples from a particular dam for several years without incident. Then one day, out of the blue, one of the team was stopped by a supervisor from a different department and asked what he was doing in the area. He was asked whether he had undertaken an induction for the area, to which our employee replied that we had been sampling that area for years without ever being told that an induction was required. The matter was reported to the*
>
> *>>*

person responsible for both our contract and ensuring that all personnel were inducted correctly. Under no circumstances was he going to take any responsibility, and he even sent a written "warning" to our company about working on site without the correct inductions.

No matter that we had never been told of such an induction, he had been signing us in and out for his entire tenure at the site, and we had absolutely no means of finding out if any inductions other than what we had were required. Judiciously, we decided not to escalate the matter—even though we had a perfect right to do so—as it would almost certainly have meant the end of our contract. And that is another lesson—knowing when to take issue with a complaint and when to withdraw without damage. Our team undertook the required induction, and we are still working at that site over a decade later.

However, there is one underlying theme in this, and all these case studies, which will be explained in the next chapter.

It's All About Reducing Their Risk

As you can see from the tier diagram (page 22) and our discussion about the supermarket, there are many places where the supply chain could break, and in the complex undertakings of a huge company, the managers and buyers for big businesses really don't want things to go wrong. These organisations may have billions of dollars at stake, so they try to ensure that every single company and person in that long supply chain knows exactly what their job is, and that they can do it properly, safely, and continuously—without micro-management.

Right, there is the one underlying thing that you need to understand if you're going to be successful as a supplier to large organisations. **They hate risk**.

That is why supplying to large organisations requires a lot more work and preparation than supplying to most other customers—**they want to reduce their risk**.

Big organisations hate risk. Their priority is to eliminate risk from their supply chain.

Large companies do very sophisticated risk analyses, and have flocks of lawyers who are all deployed to ensure that any risk to the company is minimised. **The company will be looking at all aspects of your business to identify where things could go wrong.** This includes your occupational health and safety record, environmental policies, workplace harmony (e.g., is your workforce likely to go on strike?), finances, and so on.

If you can understand that, and use that knowledge to demonstrate convincingly that your small business is not going to be the weak link in their supply chain, you're already ahead of any competitor who hasn't been able to give them the same level of comfort.

Therefore, the better you can prepare your company and demonstrate that you are **not adding to their risk**, especially given their sometimes near-death experiences during Covid-19, the greater the likelihood there is of you getting work.

---

*The better you can prepare your company and demonstrate that you are **not adding to their risk**, the greater the likelihood there is of you getting work.*

Chapter 5
Why Would They Buy from Me?

Businesses are often classified as one of two types: those that deal directly with other businesses as their customers (Business to Business or B2B), and those that supply product or services directly to the end users of those products or services (Business to Customer or B2C).

Business to Business and Business to Customer relationships are different. You must understand these differences because selling to another business is not the same as selling directly, say, to a large number of retail customers. If you're selling wholesale clothing to stores, your relationship with those stores will be vastly different to the relationship between those stores and their customers—the buyers and wearers of those jeans and jackets—in terms of marketing, customer shopping experiences (including in-store and online purchasing), and terms of trade.

But in reality, every B2B transaction comes down to a H2H transaction—human-to-human.

In the words of one of the business owners I interviewed while preparing to write this book: "It boils down to relationships. If they like you, they buy."

I have just spent several pages explaining how big buyers hate risk, and this is the reason they ask their suppliers to use the equivalent of a small forest in paperwork before they will do business with them. If it's that much of a problem, why would they do business with you anyway?

The process of on-boarding a new supplier is long and arduous, and big companies need to be convinced that the effort of having you qualified as a supplier is worth it. Many will avoid it wherever possible. However, **it turns out that there are actually several very good reasons why a big company would deliberately choose a small company such as yours over a larger competitor.**

Price

Price is definitely a double-edged sword. Depending on a host of factors, the price offered by a small business may be either lower or higher than a large competitor. There are several factors that work towards small businesses being able to offer lower prices, and one of the biggest is the lack of corporate overheads. One day, if you are wandering around the CBD of a major city with nothing to do, take a detour through the lobby of the headquarters of a major multinational company. You will be impressed by the spaciousness, the modern statues and artworks, the expensive surfaces, and the general feeling of opulence. Yes, I am completely aware that office design and layout is important for workplace health and productivity, but I can't help thinking that an excessive amount of marble is just a tad ostentatious. And that opulence comes at a high cost that has to be recovered somewhere—usually in the prices that company charges.

There is usually no such luxury for the small business owner; we can often charge a lower price and still be highly profitable because we don't have to cover the cost of a corporate head office and all that marble.

Location

Location can also provide a competitive advantage for your small business if you are located closer to your customer than your competitors.

First, **your travel and transport charges will be lower**, especially if your competitors have to fly in goods and/or personnel to do a job.

Second, **your location is working to lower your big customer's risk**. Your local presence affords the customer a shorter supply line, with fewer chances for interruption. This is the greatest opportunity for small business owners now that we have all experienced the effects of a global pandemic—particularly for critical supplies. If you, as a local supplier, can provide permanent access to a critical supply, you have a much better chance of being selected as a supplier.

Government Legislation and Procurement Guidelines

Sometimes, governments may introduce legislation that requires big companies to use small businesses. That is, the organisation must engage, or at least attempt to engage, local suppliers before offering contracts to other companies. This has the effect of forcing the large company to actively engage with local small companies (as opposed to branch offices of other large companies). For example, NSW Government agencies must give first consideration to purchasing from a SME for any contract up to $3 million in value. The UK government has a target of having one-third of its own purchases coming from small business[2]. The US government has "set-asides", where business opportunities are open only to small businesses.

The Australian state of Queensland has a Queensland Charter for Local Content which mandates "full, fair and reasonable opportunities" for local suppliers, which will often be small businesses, to bid for government procurements. However, when you are looking at local content policies, make sure you check how "local" is defined. In the Queensland Charter for Local Content, for example, local industry is formally defined as Australian and New Zealand small and medium sized enterprises (SMEs).

Local content policies can be a real boost for small businesses though, and many local councils have introduced a local weighting that favours local companies when tenders are evaluated. We will look more closely at this topic in Section 6.

Social Licence to Operate

Purchasing locally also contributes positively to the big company's **social licence to operate (SLO)**. This licence isn't one that big companies can buy or apply for like a driving licence though. The SLO is intangible, and arises from the attitudes, opinions, and beliefs of the host community. It is the acceptance of the company or project by the local community and other stakeholders, and can be damaged very quickly in the face of corporate misbehaviour or perceived wrongdoing. Positively engaging with local businesses and the host community, and keeping them informed, goes a long way to ensuring that a big company retains its SLO.

---

2   Unfortunately, the government is falling short of this target. As at October 2022, only 21% of spending was with SMEs. One wonders what effect the global Covid-19 pandemic may have had on those spending patterns.

Social Responsibility

End consumers are becoming more and more sensitive to where their purchases come from and how they are produced. Consequently, all companies (including yours) must be cognisant of their **corporate social responsibility (CSR)**. That is, every company (and its employees) have responsibilities beyond just making a profit; they also have a responsibility to take into account how its actions affect broader society and the environment. Corporate activities such as polluting the environment, underpaying or mistreating employees, unethical behaviour, breaking the law, etc. Collectively, these responsibilities are referred to with the acronym **ESG – Environmental, Social, and Governance**. ESG infringements will be noticed by end consumers, who will take action to punish the perceived anti-social behaviour.

Research shows that all business stakeholders (consumers, employees and investors) hold businesses accountable, and will take action based on their beliefs and values.

Approximately two-thirds will buy from, advocate for, work for, or invest in a company that agrees with their values and beliefs.[3] We've all seen the stories in the media where an international brand is found to be using slave labour or sub-standard manufacturing facilities in their supply chain, and suffered a public backlash as a result.

Nike, the well-known international sports brand, found out the hard way that consumers really are interested in more than the price and style of their sports equipment. Back in 1991, stories started circulating that employees making Nike products in Indonesian factories were working in terrible conditions. Nike had contracted manufacturing to an Indonesian-based supplier, creating a supply chain not controlled by them. Initially, Nike denied that there was a problem, but a campaign to boycott Nike products started to gain

---

3   https://www.edelman.com/trust/2022-trust-barometer

ground, resulting in significant financial and public relations damage to the company. The terrible working conditions were created by the Indonesian manufacturer, but Nike copped the flack and the consumer backlash.

The COVID-19 pandemic gave us more recent examples of this. World-wide, governments flooded economies with billions of dollars so that businesses could continue operating and employees could afford necessities to live. Several Australian companies paid increased dividends and bonuses when government stimulus packages (such as the JobKeeper scheme) were issued to help keep employees on the books.

British entrepreneur and founder of the Virgin brand Richard Branson requested UK taxpayer assistance, despite not having paid tax in the UK for 14 years.

US lawmakers requested five large corporations return their share of $50 million taken that was meant for small businesses. Apparently, only one returned the money.

An even more dramatic example is the Deepwater Horizon oil spill in 2010. An explosion on the Deepwater Horizon offshore oil drilling rig in the Gulf of Mexico in April 2010 resulted in the deaths of 11 people and almost 5 million barrels of oil spilling into the environment. The incident is considered to be the largest marine oil spill in history and the effects on the environment will be felt for generations. Most people remember this incident and refer to it as the BP oil disaster or the BP oil spill. BP was certainly the company at the top of that particular supply chain and was apportioned partial blame in the subsequent enquiries, but it was found that one of the central causes of the explosion was defective cement used by Transocean (the rig owner and operator) and Halliburton (a contractor). So while there were several companies found to be at fault, the oil giant suffered the most significant damage. Their corporate reputation was severely damaged and they were required to pay US$18.7 billion in fines.

More recently, the reputation (and value) of serial entrepreneur Elon Musk and the companies he controls have come under fire. Musk became embroiled in a messy takeover of the social media platform Twitter in April 2022 while championing free speech "absolutism". This doctrine permits any and all public comments on the platform, no matter the truth or toxicity of said comments. The price of shares in other companies he controls fell heavily as investors withdrew support in the face of Musk's public pronouncements.

More recently, Russia's invasion of Ukraine in February 2022 prompted consumer and investor action. These groups combined to pressure some 450 international companies to pause or completely abandon their operations in Russia. For example, the Marriott hotel group said that restrictions by Western countries "make it impossible for Marriott to continue to operate or franchise hotels in the Russian market".[4]

Protecting their CSR ESG reputation is the reason most large buyers ask what can seem to be extremely intrusive questions about your industrial relations record, environmental performance, any outstanding legal claims, etc. In fact, you may find that your potential customer wants information from your suppliers even further down the supply chain. You may choose not to answer these questions, but be aware that by electing to do so, you will almost certainly be ruling yourself out of contention for any work. The fact that your big prospective customer is asking these questions usually means that CSR is being taken seriously at a high level, and they are not prepared to leave themselves open to any possible doubt. CSR may be taken seriously to avoid any costs rather than out of a genuine desire to be a responsible corporate citizen, but the effect on your business is the same.

---

4   https://www.nytimes.com/article/russia-invasion-companies.html

In the real world ...
On January 14, 2013, the Food Safety Authority of Ireland announced that horse DNA had been detected in beef burger patties sold in supermarkets. The contaminated products were sold in the major supermarket chains (Tesco, Aldi, Asda, etc.) under some well-known brand names (Findus) as well as house brands. Shocking as that was, things were to get worse. As investigations were launched in the UK and across Europe, some products were found to contain up to 100% horse meat instead of beef. While these discoveries were culturally objectionable (eating horse meat is not a tradition of most Western cultures), there was a potentially serious health threat. Certain drugs are prohibited in animals bred for human consumption as they are, well, not good for humans. These drugs could have made their way into the human food chain via the illegally introduced horse meat.

Of course, there were extensive investigations into how this could have happened. Corruption and cost-cutting provided the motivation for the fraud, but very long supply chains offered the opportunity. Companies and supermarkets simply didn't ask enough questions.

In the words of one journalist covering the unfolding story in February 2013, "If a Swedish company makes a lasagne by using French, Dutch and Cypriot firms to source Romanian meat via Luxembourg, then the supply chain is long enough to be corruptible."[5]

---

5   Fraser Nelson, "Slavery, Not Horse Meat, Is the Real Scandal on Our Doorstep," *The Telegraph*, February 14, 2013, http://www.telegraph.co.uk/foodanddrink/foodanddrinknews/9870692/Slavery-not-horse-meat-is-the-real-scandal-on-our-doorstep.html.

Responsiveness

If you've ever tried to get a decision out of a government department, you will identify with this. It seems that at least five layers of bureaucracy are required for any decision at all—including the colour of the paperclips. Big companies are no different. Meanwhile, in small business land, the business owner has complete control over their own decisions. I often make a point of this when I present at conferences or workshops and my presentation follows that of a big company or government representative. Inevitably, their first one, two or even three slides are filled with disclaimers, usually in very small text so that nobody can be held responsible for saying anything. When I begin my presentation, I point out that I have no disclaimers. I am in complete control of what I say, and am responsible for every word. Therefore, I can make a decision that will help my customers immediately, as the only person I have to confer with is myself.

Translated into practical outcomes, this means that, in the same time your big competitor needs to fill out forms and wait to get approval to buy a plane ticket, your company will have been able to contact the client, visit them if necessary, and have the whole problem solved. You as a small business owner can jump into action and start getting things done, all while your competitor is still waiting for approval to leave their office.

Many big buyers that I have spoken and worked with also appreciate the fact that the person they have contact with will actually be doing the work—or at least is not too far removed from it. One of my big company contacts confided to me one day over a cup of coffee that he preferred to deal with smaller suppliers. In his experience, large suppliers will put together a proposal (often using a specialised bid team), and identify their top-shelf employees as the project contact/manager. This may be Professor Someone, or Dr. Someone Else. Once the work is performed, the professor, doctor, or senior consultant is brought in for a project briefing where the answer to every question related to the project is, "I'm not sure; I'll have to talk to the project team." That is code for "We put a couple of graduates on the job, and they did the work and wrote the report."

In the words of one large buyer, *"The people who pitched the business were the same people who would be doing the work. That was key for us."*

Innovation

Small businesses have a distinct competitive advantage in being innovative, and big companies know it. I have seen it time and again, where a small business creates an innovative solution that just works and (more importantly) allows the bigger customer to get on with doing their own business, profitably.

Innovation isn't just about technology, geeks, iPads and software though. Innovation is coming up with better ways to solve somebody's problem, and small businesses are willing to change in order to grow. Their thinking teams or design people are more accessible to each other, and likely have more time to explore new ideas or ways to do something better, too.

> **In the real world …**
> The work that one small company was performing for their large client involved the regular transport of specialised glass bottles. They were packed in special cardboard boxes, made and partitioned to exactly fit a standard number of bottles.
>
> However, the transport company employees seemed to have made a sport of destroying the boxes, and usually at least some of the bottles inside. Boxes would be left
>
> >>

sitting in water so the bottom fell out, or have forklift spears driven through their middle. This became a source of immense annoyance, not to mention cost, to both the small company and their client.

After several prototypes, the innovative small business owner came up with a clever, low tech, but extremely effective solution—plastic milk crates lined with thin polyethylene cutting boards cut to size, and foam rubber to create the partitions. It doesn't sound pretty—and it wasn't. But it was effective. Breakages stopped completely. There was a small increase in freight costs because the milk crates were heavier, but this was more than offset by the fact that the specialised bottles weren't being smashed continually.

Chapter 6
What Would Prevent Them Buying from Me?

Now that I have outlined the reasons why your potential big client would buy from you, I also need to point out the reasons they might not.

Risk

We have already examined the issue of risk in supply chains, and why big organisations will do everything they can to eliminate it. In the theoretical supermarket supply chain that we used as an example earlier (page 33), there's a risk to the supermarket. There's a risk that one of the tiers in the supply chain will experience a problem—a link in the supply chain fails. And we all know what happens when a link in a chain breaks—things don't go well. There's no steak in the meat section, and the customers are very, very unhappy. Remember all those empty supermarket shelves (and even fights in the aisles) in 2020 during the Covid-19 pandemic?

But risk in the supply chain for a large organisation isn't just the risk of non-supply. Risk to the big buyer comes in several forms, and they want to eliminate all of them. Your potential customer is also worried that you won't be able to supply on time—when they need it. They also lose sleep over whether you will be able to supply the same product or service to the same standard every time.

Can you be consistent?

Consistency is Not Negotiable

All these concerns come together in an acronym that you will hear quite often when you deal with large organisations: **DIFOT**, delivered in full, on time. There's usually a "Q" added on as well so it becomes delivered in full, on time, with quality.

DIFOTQ = delivered in full, on time, with quality.

The "Q" in DIFOTQ doesn't mean the best available. It means fit for purpose and consistent. By this definition, McDonald's produces the best quality burgers. Before you throw this book away in disgust, let me explain. I know that there are millions of places where you can buy a burger that is infinitely more delicious than a Big Mac. But is that delicious burger exactly the same, every time you order it? Would that burger taste the same if you bought it in New York, Sydney, or Copenhagen? Most probably not, but the Big Mac will be the same wherever you choose to go. That is the meaning of quality. The Big Mac is fit for purpose (it's a food source in the form of a burger), and every one is the same (consistency).

And this is how your larger competitors often win contracts over you. Their larger size and capacity allows them to provide the consistency that supply chains demand. It may be consistently inferior than your small business can provide, but it is consistent, and they can deliver every time.

Your big competitors can offer consistency. Their offering may be consistently inferior to yours, but it is consistent.

Let's compare the large supermarket we were talking about before with the local farmers' market. There is, say, a farmer who brings her fruit and vegetables to the market. The farmer has the best tomatoes you've ever tasted—they are ripened on the plant, allowing all the natural sugars and flavours to fully develop; picked and packed on the day by the farmer or her small team of workers; and sold only a few kilometres from the farm where they grew. They are completely unlike the tomatoes you can buy at the supermarket. Even though they're the same variety, the supermarket-bought ones could be substituted as the cricket ball for a test match.

Naturally, you will make a regular trip to the farmers' market to buy such a superior product. But at the end of the tomato-growing season, there is no more to be had—the local farmer simply can't supply any more. At this point, the supermarket is still selling tomatoes, but you are purchasing your tomatoes from the end of a very long supply chain. These tomatoes are from somewhere far away, and they were picked while still green so that they could make the long journey to your suburban supermarket before overripening or going rotten. It's simply not the same eating experience as the tomatoes from the local farmer. But it is consistent—you can still have tomatoes in your salad and sandwiches all year round.

And so it is with all large companies—the assurance of consistent supply at a given quality is important. There is a place for your niche product—and we will be talking at length about that later in this book—but competing with a big competitor who can offer consistency and reliability is a hurdle you must be willing to overcome.

You May Pose a Financial Risk

The risk of non-supply, or of providing sub-standard goods or services, is not the only risk that all the links in the supply chain pose to a large organisation. If any one of their suppliers collapses due to financial distress, a large organisation's supply chain will be interrupted. In our hypothetical supermarket, that means no steak in the meat section and frustrated customers. Not only will they have very unhappy customers, but the supermarket will have to expend considerable time and money finding an alternative reliable supplier.

Consequently, most big companies will put your company under a microscope and forensically examine your corporate entrails searching for weaknesses. They may ask you for your company's past financials so they can assess your financial health. Some will go so far as to ask for details of your financial arrangements with your bank or other providers of credit—whether you have lines of credit in place or other sources of funding, for instance.

Some of the questions you are asked may not even be appropriate for a small business such as yours. The problem here is that large companies establish vendor management systems that are tailored to companies much bigger than yours (Tier 1 or 2 companies), or even in different industries. They then copy and paste, and use the same questionnaires for every supplier—big or small—and regardless of industry sector.

In some cases, you may find yourself struggling to even understand what the questions mean, let alone whether to answer them or not.

There is also another potential, and not-so-noble, reason your prospective big customer might ask you for such detailed information. Knowledge of your financial position also gives them knowledge of your profitability, and this can be used against you by squeezing your rates or payment terms, to your disadvantage. Some go as far as specifying a maximum profit margin percentage.

No. Personnel Required	Wage / Hour	Onward Cost/Hour						Personnel Allowances - Other							Wage / Hour	Allowances - other specify	Profit	Charge
		Superannuation Guarantee	Company Payroll Tax	Workers Compensation	Other Insurances	Long Service Leave	Management | Admin	Uniforms & PPE	Induction. Train. Development	Accommodation | Meals	Corporate Expenses	Travel | Vehicles	Equipment | Tools	Overhead | Premises	Fixed Machinery			Profit Margin %	Hourly Rate

Large companies may ask their suppliers to fill in spreadsheets similar to this one, detailing their costs and profit margins. While companies use these to check that a supplier doesn't pose a financial risk, sometimes they're used to check if the supplier is making "too much" profit!

If you haven't had such a request previously, this can be very confronting, and your first reaction will be, "What the heck do they want that for? It's none of their business!" Or something like that.

Of course, you always have the option of refusing to supply such information. If you are a private company, this information is, correctly, private, and you may decide that the protection of your private financial data is of utmost importance. In the case of a tender response (see Section 6), however, not supplying the information will most probably rule your company out of contention completely, so you must consider that when making your decisions. Your company contact (see Chapter 31) may be of assistance to you in navigating your proposal through the procurement department without full disclosure if your goods and services are important enough to them. In other words, they need you to help them look good.

Systems and Processes Above What's Necessary for SME Functionality

Every small business owner knows that they should have their business systems documented. It's a bit like going for a daily walk. You know you should do it, but you probably don't—until the doctor tells you that you are going to die unless you do.

The pre-qualification process for many large buyers is long and complex, as we have already seen. Proving that you have robust business systems that will ensure your quality, consistency of delivery, and cost measurements is a key part of that pre-qualification. Their standards are set high, and they expect those standards to be maintained. Seven out of ten business owners tell me that "understanding the requirements" is the main hurdle to securing business contracts with big corporations. They said that they just had to "work out for themselves how to comply with corporate requirements, and implement them the best they could manage".

I won't spend too much time here talking about business systems as there is an entire section in this book on the subject (see Section 4). Be aware, though, that this is one of the most-cited reasons why big companies won't deal with you and your small business colleagues. You will have to be able to demonstrate convincingly that you have developed and implemented business policies and procedures that will ensure you can meet their requirements for:

- occupational health and safety
- environmental impact
- quality
- compliance with any qualifications, standards, etc.
- on-time supply
- cost competitiveness
- resources—do you have the required people/machinery?
- continuous improvement and innovation

Internal Corporate Policies

Sometimes, big companies have their own internal policies that actively prevent them from engaging you as a supplier. The most common reason is that somewhere, someone further up the decision tree implemented a system that locks in certain suppliers. They may have a preferred supplier list of suppliers who have already completed a pre-qualification assessment. That way, the big company is sure that the businesses they approach to do any work for them have all the qualifications required, and are deemed to be the best possible potential suppliers. I will talk more about preferred supplier lists later in this book (page 199), so don't fret if you don't understand them just yet.

These preferred supplier lists can be a source of immense frustration for small business owners. They preclude them from even having a chance to win contracts.

In the words of one small business owner I interviewed, "We … want to be given the opportunity to tender. We don't ever find out about contracts coming up".[6]

A big company may also do a deal with a particular supplier that covers a particular area—local, state-wide, national, or even international. Once the deal is done, all other potential suppliers, including small and local companies, are locked out for the duration of the deal. While this can ensure lower prices for the big buyer, there can be problems with the implementation of such deals.

> **In the real world …**
> A multinational mining company did a deal with an international laboratory services company, ensuring that all laboratory samples would be sent to their laboratories.
>
> >>

---

6   Ana Maria Esteves, Mary Anne Barclay, Daniel Samson, and David Brereton, *Local SME Participation in the Supply Chains of Australian Mining, Oil and Gas Companies* (Brisbane: Centre for Social Responsibility in Mining, University of Queensland, 2009).

> *The deal also included the collection of those samples—a service that was traditionally done by another contractor. The incumbent contractor was summarily dismissed and replaced by a person from the big company. The new arrangements lasted precisely one month before the mining company requested the original contractor to resume their previous contract. The replacement personnel had neither the equipment nor the skills to complete the work required.*

Earlier, I referred to **EPC (engineering, procurement and construction) and EPCM (engineering, procurement and construction management)** arrangements, where the big company at the top of the supply chain gives one large contract to a single Tier 1 company. This typically happens where there is a single, large project to be completed. That Tier 1 company then assumes all the risk for the completion of the project. Therefore, they are much more likely to stick with their own suppliers with whom they have an already established relationship, rather than take a risk on a new, small company like yours. Thus, the EPC/EPCM model, which suits the project proponent, may have the effect of locking out small or local suppliers from the supply chain.

"Teddy Bear Blanket" Syndrome

"Teddy bear blanket" syndrome is our term for the big company (or at least somebody responsible for procurement) acting a little bit timid, and sticking with a comfort level they are happy with—like a child does with a security blanket. Even when the child's parent offers them a new, cleaner, softer, better, warmer blanket, the child still wants their old blanket, because it is familiar and they feel secure.

Similarly, a procurement manager chooses a larger supplier over your offering, even though your proposal may be superior in all respects—cost, service, reliability, capabilities—everything. The company selects the larger supplier because they believe that it offers better security, even though your insurances are equal, and are unwilling to try anything different and new, even if it is better, softer, warmer, etc.

This problem is related to the incumbent's advantage, which we will talk about in Chapter 40.

Maybe You're Invisible

I once had a small business owner tell me that Facebook was the work of the Devil. No, he wasn't particularly religious—he was merely expressing what many small business owners think: "Facebook is frightening, and is to be avoided at all costs." Since then, the variety and number of possible marketing channels has only increased. To digital non-natives (anyone born in the 1980s), the result is even more confusion.

Unfortunately, this attitude is not going to get you many big customers. From my own research, I know that 65% of small businesses say that "getting noticed" is the main hurdle to securing business contracts with corporations.

But there are two sides to any story, and big companies have their own perspective. They report that often, even if they do want to find and engage small suppliers, they lack professionalism in their marketing, and are therefore all but invisible.

The two main deficiencies cited by large purchasers are:
- no website, and
- no professional email address (Gmail and Hotmail are not considered to be professional email addresses).

In the current internet age, not having a website is commercial death. Over 85% of customers consult online reviews before purchasing a product[7]. Globally, 81% of potential customers will look for products and services online. Just over three-quarters of them are going on to purchase in an online store[8]. And yet, as recently as 2021, four in ten small businesses did not have a website at all[9].

So, if you do not take anything else away from reading this book, at least start with getting your business a website.

I will be talking more about your digital presence in Section 5.

Perception of Lack of Customer Service

Many large businesses have the attitude that small businesses are not committed to excellent customer service. I know that you are, because you wouldn't be reading this book if you weren't on the lookout for ways to make your business improve and grow. However, not every small business owner shares your passion and, unfortunately, we are all tarred by the same brush as a result.

Some of the most commonly cited customer service issues that big companies have with small businesses are:

- slow response times for queries, proposals, quotes, and service requests
- slow or delayed delivery due to poor logistics management
- poor communications, because a small business often lacks sufficient staff, and the owner is tied up working "in the business" and can't be contacted
- negative attitude towards providing a service that is any different

---

7   https://www.redsearch.com.au/resources/local-seo-statistics-australia/
8   https://www.savvy.com.au/australias-online-shopping-behaviour-report-2022/#:~:text=81.5%25%20are%20searching%20online%20for,years%20between%202017%20and%202022
9   https://digitaleconomy.pmc.gov.au/sites/default/files/2021-07/digital-economy-strategy.pdf

to what they are accustomed to giving
- high staff turnover, meaning a lack of continuity of available staff

I personally find the last one very strange. In my 26 years of owning a business, I have seen a much higher staff turnover within my big clients than in any of the small businesses I know! However, for the astute small business owner, this list provides a very clear insight into how they can claim a competitive advantage—even over their larger rivals, because even they drop the ball on customer service more often than they would like to admit.

Two iconic Australian brands spring to mind as examples. The mere thought of having to contact Telstra is enough to put my blood pressure into the stratosphere. I know that I will have to write off at least one day that will be dedicated to a combination of waiting on hold and being transferred from department to department. Qantas, and airlines in general, plumbed the depths of customer service and responsiveness as they restarted scheduled air services after Covid-19 travel restrictions were lifted. At the time of writing, I have lost my Qantas Club membership. I am not able to renew it online, and all my emails and messages have remained unanswered.

This is where we really have to shine as small businesses.

Your Price is Too High or Too Low

I know that I've already noted that price is one reason that your potential big customer will sign a contact with you—your business doesn't have to carry the cost of a shiny head office trimmed with glass and marble. However, sometimes we are more expensive, for any number of reasons. At times, one of those reasons may be that your bigger competitor (with appropriately bigger pockets) can undercut you in order to "buy" business—perhaps just to keep people employed, or sometimes as a "loss leader" strategy to gain more business and see off any competitors.

If your service is sufficiently niched and provides excellent customer service (see above), you will be better able to justify your higher prices and still successfully compete against them.

Their Financial Policies

The odd thing about your potential big customer wanting to forensically examine your financials is that their payment policies sometimes seem to be designed to make your finances worse! Research from the Australian Small Business and Family Enterprise Ombudsman (ASBFEO) shows that in Australia, seven out of 10 big businesses take more than 30 days to pay their small suppliers. One-quarter take more than 120 days to make payment.[10]

For the small business owner, this means that while there are huge rewards to be had from having a big-name customer, you must carefully consider the impact on your cash flow.

Since 30 November 2021, all Australian companies with a turnover of more than $100 million have to report their payment terms to the federal government every six months. This data is made publicly available through the Australian Government's Payment Times Reports Register.[11] So now we can see the real figures, and no longer have to rely on occasional surveys and anecdotal evidence.

Among the data they have to report, these giant companies have to declare what percentage of invoices were paid in the following time brackets:

---

10   www.asbfeo.gov.au. (n.d.). BIG BUSINESSES URGED TO 'LIFT THEIR GAME' ON PAYMENT TIMES. [online] Available at: https://www.asbfeo.gov.au/media-centre/media-releases/big-businesses-urged-lift-their-game-payment-times [Accessed 1 Mar. 2023].
11   "Payment Times Report Register," Australian Government Payment Times Reporting Regulator, https://register.paymenttimes.gov.au.

- less than 20 days
- 21–30 days
- 31–60 days
- 61–90 days
- 91–120 days
- more than 120 days

The way the data is presented makes it impossible to tell how many invoices were paid after their official due date. But without that information, I'm going to make a (very reasonable) assumption; any invoice paid after 30 days is 'late'. In other words, even if the payment terms are longer than 30 days, they shouldn't be.

Using this assumption, just over one third of invoices are being paid 'late' … so there is still a long way to go. Clearly, there is room for improvement as we pursue the 30-day payment target for all small businesses.

I used the data from the report to create this graph. It shows the breakdown of payment times reported. The story it tells is that just over half of Australia's big companies still have payment terms greater than 30 days for their small suppliers.

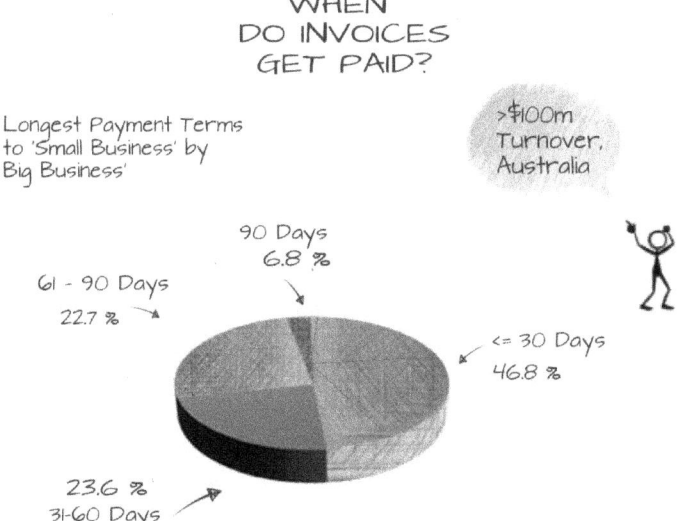

The data on the Payment Times Report Register also tells us that there are still companies that have official payment terms of over 120 days. Incredibly, 11 of these were over one year. Imagine waiting a whole year to get paid!

What use is this report to you?

Now that we have this valuable information available to us every six months, we can use it as valuable business intelligence. I know well the excitement of being contacted by a very large company about the possibility of winning some work with them. But there's a lot to think through before you leap in and sign the contract …

If you have not dealt with that company before, you won't know if they are good payers, or one of those that is going to make you wait a whole year for your money. Now you can simply open the Payment Times Register online and search for your prospective client. The report is in a spreadsheet, so searching is as simple as a quick Excel search. In seconds you will be able to see their track record and use that information to either help make your decision or negotiate better terms before the contract starts.

Chapter 7
Understanding Contracts

Purchase Orders and Contracts—Episode 1

Never work without one. *Ever!*

Purchase Orders and Contracts—Episode 2

When you finally land your big client, no doubt you will be extremely excited, and wanting to get going straight away. But don't be in a rush—there are some legal issues that you need to be aware of and attend to first.

Big organisations are bureaucratic, and any function that involves them spending money attracts a lot of attention. This is where we need to discuss ***purchase orders*** and ***contracts**.*

Purchase Orders

Once you have agreed with your big buyer on the work they want you to do and how much they will pay you, they will usually issue a ***purchase order (PO)**,* which is also sometimes called a service order

(SO). A purchase order is the document issued by a buyer that requests and authorises you to supply something—some goods or services.

Purchase orders vary greatly in the amount of detail they contain, and I've seen many variations. At a minimum, the PO will contain the name, unit price, quantity, total price, and sometimes a brief description of the goods or services that are being delivered by you. It will also show you the exact details of the entity that you must send your invoice to. **Check this carefully**—many big companies use subsidiary companies, and sending an invoice to the wrong entity will most probably delay your payment.

Some POs will go into immense detail—breaking down what they want from you into minute line-items—generally drawn from the proposal or tender documents you submitted. Others will just show a single line—perhaps the name of the project—and then refer to other documents such as your proposal or tender submission.

The PO may also set out terms and conditions—how you and the purchaser will deal with each other. As with other details, the actual PO you receive may not contain all or explicit terms and conditions; it's very common instead for POs to refer you to the organisation's website where you can download and read their standard terms and conditions. Your customer may also offer you an overall agreement that then applies to every purchase order that is subsequently issued.

It is critical that you read the terms and conditions.

At this stage, you don't actually have a contract with your prospective customer. **Only after you accept the purchase order** does a contract come into force between you and the buyer.

Contracts

The contract that has been formed between your business and the customer is a legally binding document—so it is much more than just an agreement between the two of you. A legal contract has some specific elements that you should be aware of but, sadly, many small business owners don't realise this until it is too late. It is not my intention to go into too much detail in this book about contracts—it's a whole branch of law that keeps thousands of lawyers constantly busy—but I'd like to give you enough information so you understand the relationship between yourself and your big customer.

There are not a lot of legal boundaries around purchasing—most of it is governed by contract law, which I've already referred to—so it is important that you have at least a basic knowledge of your obligations.

Essentially, there are five elements to a legally binding contract:

1. **Offer and acceptance**. You have products and services on offer. Your offer is accepted when the buyer sends you a purchase order and you agree to do the work/supply the services according to the terms and conditions (acceptance).
2. **Intention to create a legal relationship**. Offering to take your neighbour's bin out while they're on holiday has an offer and acceptance, but it is not intended to create a legally binding relationship. In a business setting, however, your terms and conditions will make it clear that you are mutually entering a legally binding relationship.
3. **Consideration**. Money or some value will be exchanged between the parties.
4. **Capacity to contract**. Both parties to the contract are free to enter into the contract. This is rarely a consideration but can introduce some problems if there is a bankruptcy involved or the person signing the contract is not authorised to act on behalf of the company.
5. **Consent**. The contract must be understood and consented to by both parties. This is an area that can create difficulties because of the power difference between the big buyer and you,

the small business owner. In many countries, governments have intervened and placed restrictions on the sorts of terms and conditions big companies can put into their standard contracts.

In 2016, legislation came into effect in Australia[12] that allowed the courts to assess whether contract terms were unfair, and to declare them void. A term is unfair and void (unenforceable) if it significantly imbalances parties' rights, is not reasonably necessary to protect the advantaged party's interests, and would cause detriment to the disadvantaged party.

The catch is that small business owners have to take action against the big company imposing unfair terms. That means approaching the courts and asking them to make a ruling. That is a huge, gaping hole in the legislation. Very, very few SMEs have either the money or the intestinal fortitude to front up for such a court case. The best they can do, which has always been my approach, is to point out the unfair terms and hope the big company agrees with you and deletes or changes them. October 2022 saw additional amendments that finally made unfair contract terms illegal and introduced financial penalties for using them[13].

The most important change makes unfair contract terms illegal in the first place. No more nonsense of putting or keeping an unfair clause in, and waiting for a small business (or the ombudsman) to call it out. Under the previous legislation, the only downside for a big company was that the offending clause was not able to be enforced. There was no penalty. Now, it is illegal to "propose, apply, or rely on" an unfair contract term. There is also a monetary penalty for breaches.

---

12   The changes were contained in the Competition and Consumer Act 2010 (Cth) (CCA).
13   *The Treasury Laws Amendment (More Competition, Better Prices) Bill 2022* amended the *Competition and Consumer Act 2010* and *Australian Securities and Investments Commission Act 200.*

To deter other potential offenders, once a contract term has been declared to be unfair, no other company can use a similar term. That will prevent having the same things presented to the courts over and over again. The number of contracts that legislation applies to has also been increased by removing the maximum contract value threshold.

What does this mean for small business owners?

When the new legislation takes effect, it will be another small step along the path of closing the power gap between small business and their big corporate customers. But that doesn't mean you can stop watching the standard form contracts presented to you for offending unfair contract terms.

It may seem that the purpose of a contract is to give all the rights to the buyer, and leave you with no rights at all. However, a contract is there to protect both parties and you, too, have rights.

Checking the Contract

Those five elements of a contract (page 53) look very simple, but once corporate lawyers get their hands on a contract, you can be sure that it will morph into pages and pages of mind-numbing gobbledegook. This is where you need your own highly competent commercial (but also friendly and not going to cost you your firstborn or body parts) lawyer to ensure that the contract terms you are agreeing to are:
- able to be met
- acceptable to you

Some contracts contain extremely onerous conditions, and even some that may be impossible to meet (a typical example of this is insurance—more on that later).

This may seem over the top, but you really should review every contract. Even when you've been working for a company for a very long time, their terms and conditions can change. You may be notified of the changes, or you may not.

If you find issues that are not acceptable to you, you need to raise them with your potential buyer before progressing. Sometimes, you will have to compromise—all negotiations involve some give and take. While the negotiating process is continuing, make sure you keep in touch with the person for whom you will be performing the work. An individual waiting to have a job completed can be advocating for you and pressing your case from within the company.

> **In the real world ...**
> Contracts for a very large multinational company I tracked over several years had new parts added to the contract throughout that time. The contract terms and conditions were attached to each purchase order rather than in an overall agreement or listed on their website, so the supplier would have had to read the entire six pages of size eight font every time they won another contract to pick up the changes.

The courts **may** declare void any obligation to perform a change that is tucked away in fine print, but it will depend on the circumstances, the type of change, and whether there is a head contract that spells out how the company will communicate changes. Remember that contracts come in all shapes and sizes, so don't be afraid to ask questions or challenge procedures that you think are unworkable.

While you are looking through the contract, there are a few things to watch out for. I emphasise that this book does not purport to give legal advice—that's what you need a lawyer for. These are some things I have seen appear in contracts that can cause problems for the unsuspecting small business owner.

Is there a no fault termination clause?

You may think that your contract is for a certain length of time, but there will always be a ***termination clause***. The termination clause will detail the circumstances under which the contract can be cancelled, and what happens if it is cancelled—payments, invoicing, etc.

This is one of the contract terms that was in the sights of the sights of the Australian Competition and Consumer Commission under the Unfair Contract laws.[14] Termination clauses like the one below, which allows the buyer to terminate the contract for no reason, but does not permit you, the supplier, to do the same, has fallen foul of the courts.

> *"Termination notice: The company may terminate the contract or any part of it by giving the service provider not less than 30 days' notice of its intention to do so."*

Check the services to be performed/scope of works

If the ***scope of works***, or what you are doing for the customer, has been copied from your original proposal or tender, **please, please, please check that it has been copied correctly**. I have seen many instances where tasks have been left out or added in. I honestly don't

---

14 See Australian Competition and Consumer Commission & Anor V Fuji Xerox Australia Pty Limited ACN 000 341 819 & Anor, Federal Court of Australia, Concise Statement NSD1156/2020, https://www.accc.gov.au/system/files/ACCC%20v%20Fuji%20Xerox_Concise%20Statement.pdf.

believe that it's malicious, but if you don't check the language, you can find yourself obligated to perform work you didn't bargain on.

> **In the real world ...**
>
> *Our consultancy company submitted a tender to do all the water testing at a particular location for a large resources company—their bores, dams, and rivers. There was no mention of the potable (drinking) water supply in the original scope of works. Our proposal was accepted, and the contract duly issued. However, when we checked the scope of works in the contract, all the potable water sampling and testing had been included. What had happened is that when the original scope of works was prepared, the drinking water part had been accidentally left out. Our proposal was accepted by someone higher up in contracts administration—probably because our price was cheaper than everyone else's; drinking water testing is very expensive as you have to test for bacteria, etc. We had to negotiate a change in the value of the contract to include the extra work, and that happened amicably in this case. However, it had the potential to be a tricky situation.*

This is another case for being very clear on exactly what it is that you are supplying to the buyer—and being sure that you are both "on the same page". Sometimes, a tender will be put out with a "fluffy" scope of works that could be interpreted in several different ways. Make sure that you explain very, very clearly exactly what your proposal includes and what it doesn't, and that your understanding is reflected in the contract.

> **In the real world ...**
>
> *A consultancy company tendered on a full environmental monitoring program for a large construction project. The tender documents were extremely vague; respondents were invited to download documents from a government website and figure out for themselves what the program entailed in order to meet the statutory requirements. These documents ran to several thousand pages. Having done this type of work for many years, the company was familiar with what the government requirements were and prepared their tender submission accordingly. They won the tender, but once it had been granted and the contract document issued, a whole new parcel of work appeared that had not been previously included. When the supplier objected, the company argued that the monitoring task required was actually a government requirement, and was therefore included in the scope of works.*

As you can see from this case study, you really do need to spell out what is and what isn't included in your tender, or at least seek to clarify what any vague statements in the tender documents mean.

Check the prices are all 100% correct

Just as you should check if the scope of works has been transcribed from your proposal documents to the contract, the same applies to the prices you have proposed. If the prices have been copied over from your proposal documents to the contract, make sure you check them. The alternative will likely involve a protracted negotiation with someone who may be on another continent or alternative time zone, and you will have to try and explain to them that their company has made a clerical error. Good luck with that.

Check the standards or quality specifications

Standards or quality specifications is another area for you to check carefully. Are there any specifications for quality standards, product specifications, etc., in the contract, and are they appropriate?

For example, there may be some engineering standards specified. If so, are they applicable to your particular industry or product? Sometimes quality standards can be inappropriate, beyond your capabilities, or even punitive. From your customer's perspective, by setting a very high bar for the specifications, they may be wasting a great deal of money by having you supply something that is way in excess of what they actually need. They may even be looking for the wrong thing entirely. This is another opportunity for you, as a flexible small business owner, to differentiate yourself by pointing this out and proposing your alternative, better solution. Very often, your larger competitors with professional bid teams that don't actually know much about the task to be performed, will simply "follow the rules", and submit a proposal for exactly what is written in the tender documents. We will spend a little more time on this in the chapter about tendering (Chapter 35). It's a big subject.

An alternative possibility is that you may be contracting for some standards that are not in your budget, or even your capabilities.

Here are some additional clauses about quality and specifications that I have seen appear in contracts.

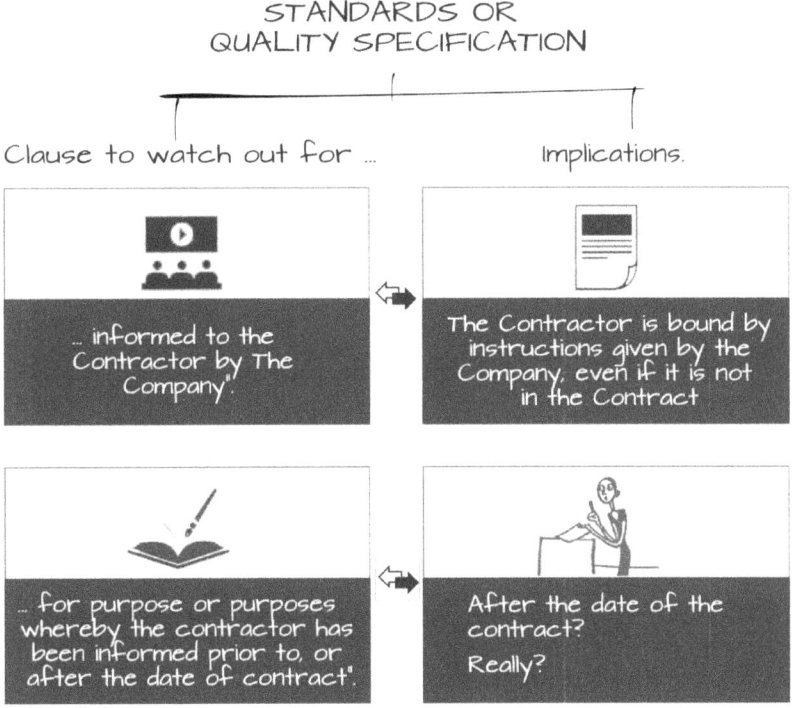

Are there time limits?

Is there a time limit on when you have to do the work or provide the goods? Is there a time limit on when you have to submit your claims?

Most contracts will specify time limits—that work or goods have to be delivered within a certain time frame. Some have additional terms that include a time limit on claims—that you must submit your claims for payment (invoices) within a certain number of days. From your big customer's point of view, they need to get their payments made for their own cash flow planning, so they don't want to have liabilities outstanding. It is always best practice to get your invoices done as quickly as possible, but these clauses are certainly an added incentive.

Are there clear directions?

Can your customer direct you as to how you will perform the services? If so, can you accept this obligation?

Your potential customer is concerned about quality and consistency and may include a clause in the contract to make sure they get exactly what they want.

An example is:

> "XYZ Pty Ltd. may in its absolute discretion within the general scope of services and from time-to-time issue directions … as to the method or manner of performing the services and the time or times with which the services or **any** part are to be commenced, performed or completed, and such directions must be complied with by the contractor. Any direction given by XYZ shall not in any way reduce or lessen any of the contractor's duties, obligations or liabilities except to the extent expressly contained in the direction or necessarily arising from the direction."

If you are providing a professional service, or you have a proprietary process, you will need to consider whether you can **accept the risk of having an external party tell you how to do your job**. This is certainly another point you need to discuss with your lawyer.

Insurance and indemnities

Do you have the required insurance? Are you being asked to insure anyone else as well as yourself?

This part of the contract is the one that can cause the most angst. And it is the clause which causes most small businesses to expose themselves to enormous risk, without even realising it.

If something goes wrong, **this means you have the liability and are obligated to fix it**. Liability is the legal term for "you're in trouble".

General provisions relating to indemnities and liabilities should be carefully considered and reworded because they distort the legal obligations normally found when parties deal with each other.

"Indemnity" is another legal word that is bandied around freely in contracts. If you "indemnify" your customer, you agree to compensate them for any loss or damage that happens because of the work you do (or don't do), or if the products you supply aren't "fit for purpose". So, if you're supplying pencil sharpeners, you probably aren't at too much risk. But if you are supplying a vital component for a space shuttle, the consequences of your screwing up can be very large indeed.

Consequently, big customers are keen to move as much of the liability for any screw-ups onto you—the supplier. This shifting of responsibility shows up in the indemnities clauses of contracts. For example, do you have insurance to cover your own employees or subcontractors working for you on this project in case of an accident that someone might get sued for?

In 2018, Australian-grown strawberries were being found with needles in them, which in at least one case was deliberate sabotage by an employee who was packing the fruit. In a situation like this, the worst-case scenario would be a child suffering severe harm. The parent's target for action would be the supermarket, then the supplier. The parents would ultimately seek redress from the farmer, not the supermarket. The lawyers acting for the parents would be seeking to discover what assets and/or insurance the farmer had. I mentioned before that the way both parties deal with each other under a contract is the subject of a whole branch of law—contract law. Contract law has been built up over centuries, largely based on the English common law system. The clauses that we often find in big company contracts can distort this relationship and attempt to impose different obligations than would normally apply under contract law.

A typical indemnity clause will look like the following:

"... shall indemnify XYZ Pty Ltd., its related bodies corporate and their respective directors, officers, employees, agents and contracts (other than the contractor and its personnel) against any loss or damage they suffer as a result of the failure by the contractor or its personnel to comply with any reasonable instructions or directions given by XYZ Pty Ltd. under clause XX)."

The contractor will be liable for, and will indemnify the principal and keep the principal indemnified from and against any liability and/or any loss or damage of any kind whatsoever, arising directly or indirectly from: [A long list of things that could possibly go wrong]."

Effectively, what this clause is asking you to do is to take on the cost of anything that goes wrong for the buyer. Under contract law, each party to a contract has obligations to not breach the contract. This type of clause dramatically expands the obligations your company would normally have. If you agree to this clause, you would be fully liable for any damage caused to the company, no matter whose fault it is, except to the extent that the damage was caused directly by the company's wilful misconduct or gross negligence. **Gross negligence has a different legal meaning to plain old negligence.** Normally the buyer would be liable to the extent that their negligence contributes to the damages.

While the likelihood of your big customer taking action against you may be small, the consequences could be enormous if they ever did. I have even seen mental illness included in the list of things you are indemnifying them against. If your customer is a huge multinational, indemnifying the mental health of a few hundred thousand of their employees may be a bridge too far for your insurance company.

Along with clauses asking for indemnities, there will often be a clause requiring you to "name the principal as a named co-insured":

> *"The contractor will ensure that all policies of insurance required to be taken out by it under this agreement (other than the insurance noted in clause xxx) include the principal as a named co-insured."*

Generally, your insurer will insist that these types of clauses be deleted, and it is imperative that you get your insurance broker to look over the contract before you sign it. I have not come across an insurance company yet that will extend your insurance coverage to your big customers. Most insurers will agree to have the buyer noted on the insurance policy, but not to add them as a co-insured.

Indemnity clauses

Indemnity clauses are a real problem. They are appearing more and more frequently in contracts, often with no apparent reason, and no real understanding of their full impact or consequences for suppliers. (I have seen indemnity clauses that actually contradict themselves.) Hence, your requests to alter these clauses will often be met with reluctance. **It is up to you to decide the likelihood of something going wrong, and whether you can tolerate the risk involved.**

Another tricky indemnity clause that pops up is a provision called a ***waiver of subrogation***. This can be quite complex, but in short, it means that your insurer can't go after the buyer or their insurer to recover any damages if things go wrong. Again, it is vitally important that you check with your insurance company because many insurers will not agree to this clause.

It also pays to verify to whom the indemnity clause actually applies:

> *"Subject to clause xx, the service provider will indemnify (and will keep indemnified) the company, each end user and their respective personnel (indemnified parties) from and against all liabilities that*

> *any indemnified party suffers, sustains or incurs, arising from any one or more of the following ..."*

This clause extends your liability to other entities who are not even a party to the contract. This exposes you to unlimited consequential loss. For example, you would be liable for loss of income for "end users" if the project was delayed by any breach of contract on your part.

Some indemnity clauses have been interpreted to mean that the company doesn't even have to incur an expense before it can enforce its right of indemnity. In other words, the company can come after you even if it hasn't made any payments to correct whatever it is that you have done wrong.

> *"No requirement for expense before enforcing indemnity: It is not necessary for the company, a member of the XX group or their respective personnel to incur expense or make payment before enforcing a right of indemnity conferred by the contract."*

If you have taken out your professional indemnity insurance through an industry association, sometimes they will offer a set number of contract reviews free every year. Given the cost of legal consultancy fees, this can save you a lot of money.

Check for variations

Are variations allowed, and what must happen when a variation is raised?

A ***variation*** is what happens when the terms of the contract are changed after the contract was signed, and this is another part of the relationship between you and your customer that can be sorely tested at times. I have seen many small and medium businesses have one person on staff whose sole job is handling contract variations. This is particularly common in the construction industry.

This is also an area that has come under the scrutiny of the courts under the Australian unfair contracts legislation. I have discussed this legislation earlier (page 54). The legislation puts the spotlight on contracts where the large organisation can vary the contract unilaterally, but the small company has no power to vary the contract at all.

Generally, there will be wide powers for the large organisation to vary the contract, and very limited powers for you (if any at all), so you need to check if this is acceptable to you. You will also have to make a judgement call on what "scope creep" you will consider acceptable, and at what point you will insist upon having a formal variation made to the contract.

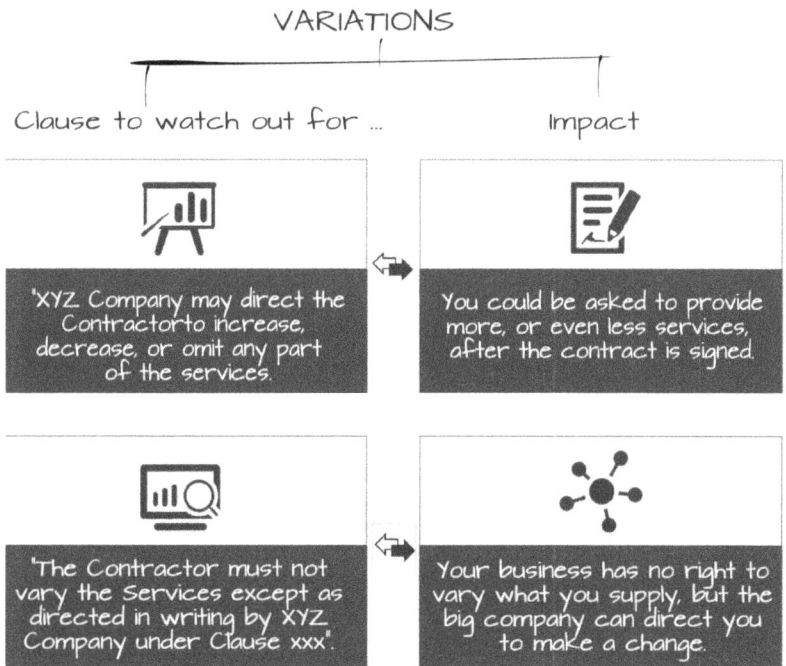

The question of intellectual property

Who owns it, and when does it get transferred to the customer?

Another particularly problematic issue in contract law is intellectual property (IP). Again, this is a whole special branch of the law, and if your products or services involve the creation of anything that could possibly involve intellectual property, seek advice from your friendly lawyer first. Once the issue of who owns IP raises its ugly head, it's already too late, and will almost certainly result in duelling lawyers. More often than not, the small business will concede defeat, simply at the prospect of a protracted and expensive legal battle. A simple clause added to the contract can clarify the issue for both parties early.

An example would be where a supplier creates a new method of solving a supply chain or design issue and offers that solution to a big company client. The supplier assumes their company owns the IP, and can offer the same or similar to another client. The big company client may be under the impression that the IP is theirs. It was created in relation to the contract being undertaken to deliver services to *them*, and therefore the IP *is theirs*.

Delays, suspension and termination

These clauses are mostly unfavourable to the supplier, and this is another area that is the subject of scrutiny under the Australian unfair contracts legislation. **Examine the clauses dealing with delays, contract suspension and termination carefully, and consider the impact they will have on your business.** Again, get legal advice if you are concerned, or you aren't sure how the clause can be varied.

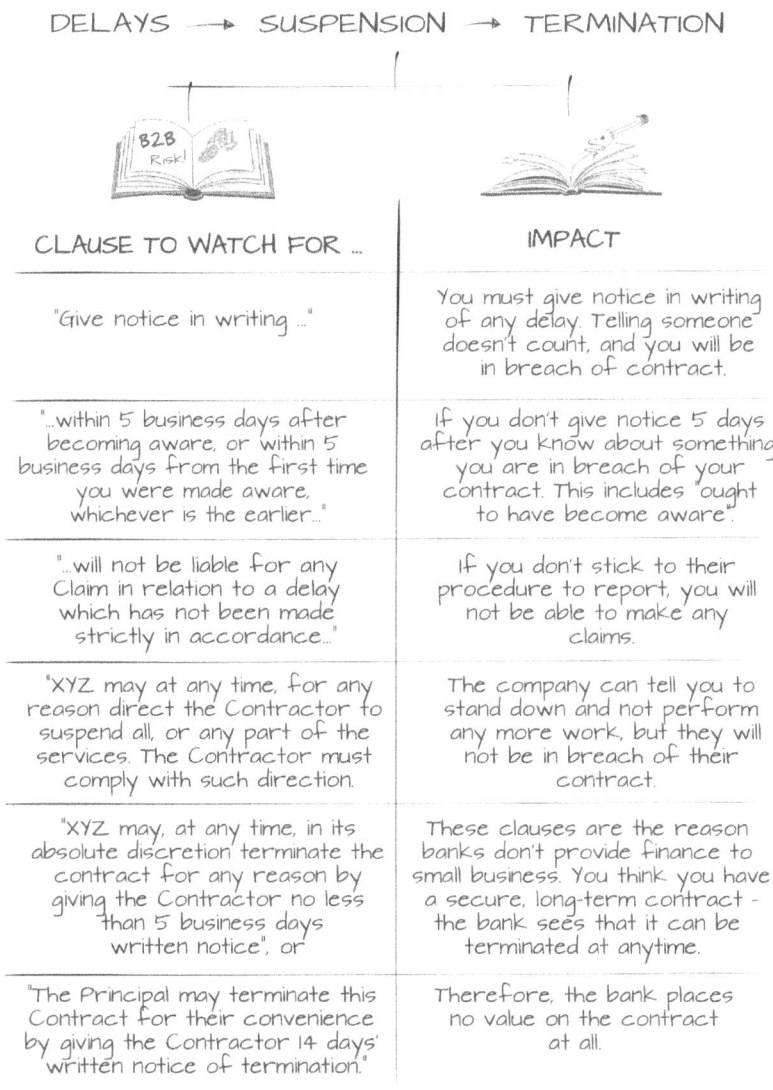

Payment terms

Always, always check the payment terms. Large companies are the worst at paying their bills on time, and often have very long payment terms. Some companies in the grocery industry, for example, will make you wait 120 days for your payment. If their payment terms are very long, you may have to discuss this with your bank and consider alternate ways to meet your financial obligations when payments are late.

Imagine your reaction if you received the following letter or email.

> *"Our future commercial arrangements with you will target a 10% reduction in prices for all goods or services that your organisation provides to XYZ operations, and a change in standard payment terms to 62 days from the receipt of a compliant tax invoice." This extract is from an actual letter received by a small supplier from a very large company.*

Long payment terms (and late payments) have been a long-lasting and constant source of conflict between small and large businesses. At long last, the federal government has taken some action. As previously discussed in Chapter 6, since January 2021, Australian companies with a turnover greater than $100 million have to lodge a report with the federal government every six months.[15] Each company has to report its shortest, standard (default), and longest payment terms to their small suppliers.

Thankfully, some of these very large companies have gone as far as having five-day payment terms for small suppliers. These are to be congratulated. Others, however, have still a way to go. As at August 2022, just over half of these companies have standard payment terms of more than 30 days.

---

15 "Payment Times Report Register," Australian Government Payment Times Reporting Regulator, https://register.paymenttimes.gov.au.

Money Well Spent

There is a saying: "There is nothing quite as expensive as a cheap lawyer." And it's true. There is a reason why there are so many specialists in contract law—**it can be fiendishly complex**. Every case will vary, with different circumstances surrounding the contracting parties, and different contract terms. With the notes from this chapter, read through the contract yourself, and highlight any clauses that concern you. Prepare a list of questions, and then contact your lawyer. Hopefully this chapter will have given you at least some clues as to where to look for potential danger in the contracts you are offered.

SECTION 2
SHOULD I PRESS THE GO BUTTON ... OR NOT?

If you truly want to step your business up to the next level by taking on contracts with large companies, the way you run your business has to change. You will have to play by a completely different set of rules.

In the previous section, I introduced the problem of the gap between you and your potential big customer. Both parties are looking at the same problems, but through their own lens—hence the disconnect.

The remainder of this book will help you to bridge that gap. However, before we launch into how to do this, there is one extremely important question that you must ask yourself: do you *really* want to supply to big organisations?

Chapter 8
Do You REALLY Want to Supply to Big Organisations?

Small business is important. It's really important.

An estimated 99% of business in Australia is classified as a small business.[16] So there are a lot of us out there across various industries, and there are likely to be tens of thousands aiming for the big contracts offered by big companies. That's a lot of paperwork, pitching, and ambition. But too often, big companies get the attention of the news media, the business media, and, particularly, government. Australia's economy is dominated by the real giants of the international corporate world—the big mining, oil and gas companies.

Here in Australia, our retail space is dominated by just a couple

---

16 The Australian Small Business and Family Enterprise Ombudsman, Small Business Counts December 2020, 2020, 7–8, https://www.asbfeo.gov.au/sites/default/files/2021-11/ASBFEO%20Small%20Business%20Counts%20Dec%202020%20v2_0.pdf.

of major companies—particularly in the grocery game. According to COSBOA, a small business lobby group, what we get to buy in this country is determined by just a handful of people—from those few major retailers.

We are now witnessing the emergence of large corporate *agribusiness* companies, as food looks to become the new boom industry following the disruptions caused by the Covid-19 pandemic.

Wherever you look, big companies seem to dominate industries.

But there in the background—constantly—are thousands and thousands of small businesses—quietly beavering away, doing their thing, and keeping the economy moving. These are the people I identify with, and the ones I have written this book for. The ones who put it all on the line to follow their idea or carve out their space in the world. As one of my business mentors, Daniel Priestly, puts it—to make their dent in the universe.

I count myself as one of these. I've started three businesses, made lots of mistakes, made both good and bad decisions, and generally learnt a whole lot of expensive lessons. I have now developed a lot of this knowledge into training programs for small business owners who are trying to take the leap of capturing one of those big contracts. (For more on these and resources for improving your odds at pitching and tendering, please check out page 227).

Bigger isn't ALWAYS better

While the big organisations I have been discussing get all the limelight, that doesn't mean they are invincible.

It might surprise you to know that 88% of companies from the 1955 Fortune 500 lists have now gone. In 2021, 18 of the largest business construction companies in Australia closed their doors, left many in their supply chains out of pocket, and thousands of people out of work.

The first two years of this decade have seen a significant number of large companies disappear off the company register, and even some of the biggest global companies in the world have closed their doors. Revlon filed for Chapter 11 (bankruptcy) in June 2022; before that Pan Am, Toys R Us, Borders, Ansett and Kodak all disappeared.

Domination is big business, but it's not always secure business either.

Educating Around This Process

It has always bemused me that our education system prepares us only to work for someone else—mostly someone else who is big. I completed my MBA during the late 1990s and early 2000s, and every single textbook was written about big companies. The texts talked about big companies, the case studies were about big companies, and we were being prepared to work for big companies. The majority of our high school graduates escape from 12 or 13 years of education with absolutely no knowledge of finance, management, or business whatsoever. Little wonder that, years later when they take the step of setting up their own business having gained a skill or trade, so many of them fail.

Things are improving though. The rapid development of technology has given rise to the opportunity for just about anyone to start a business, which is creating a step-change in how business is done. Disruption is breaking out everywhere. On our regular return trips to Africa and South East Asia, we see the impact that mobile phones have had, with solo-preneurs setting up businesses in the most unlikely places.

But the fact is that, while by far the majority of registered businesses in most developed economies are "small" (definitions vary), the majority of economic activity is still carried out by big businesses and government. As a result, the path of growth for most small business owners will, at some stage, intersect with a large buyer—a government department, a big corporation, or even a larger not-for-profit or social enterprise.

Chapter 9
The Business Journey

Before we go any further, I want to pause for a minute and ask you to think about just what you envisaged your business would be when you first started out. And to do that I want to introduce you to the concept of the ***business journey***. Two of my business mentors, Daniel Priestly and Glen Carlson of Dent[17], created this graph showing the business journey. What you're looking at here isn't new information, but I just really like the way that they have presented it.

---

17   Read about Dent's entrepreneur journey at https://www.dent.global/

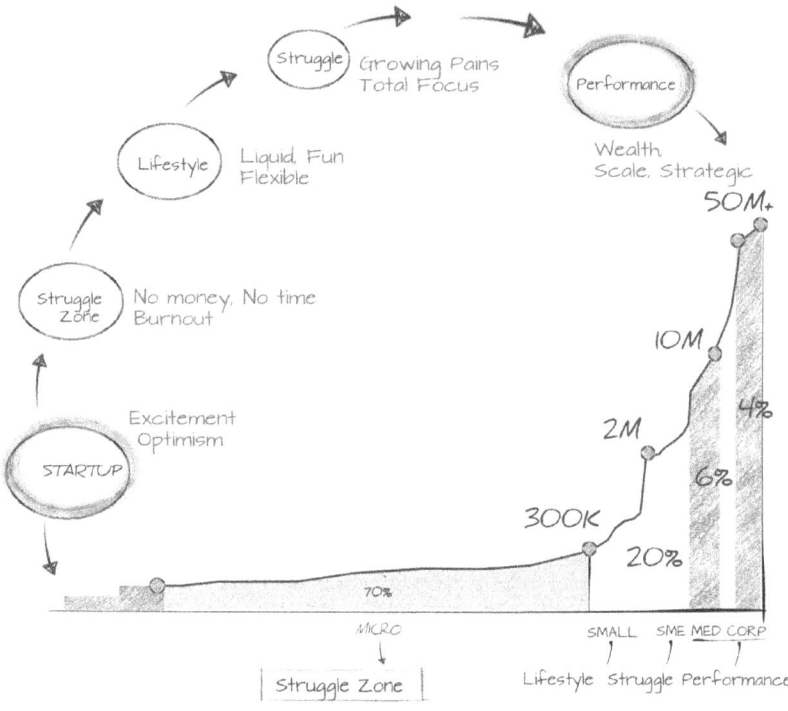

Adapted from Key Person of Influence

When you started your business, you knew what you wanted. You wanted the freedom to be your own boss—perhaps even take some time off when the kids were on school holidays. You may have even been working for a large company and they offered you the chance to go out on your own, and gave you a contract to do the work that you were already doing inside the company. Whichever way you started your business, it will have started down at the beginning of the journey, when you were excited and optimistic.

So there you are at the beginning of your business, working alone or maybe with a business partner or your life partner. Slowly but surely, the business starts to grow. You win some customers and eventually hire some team members to help you with the growing work load. This is always a huge point of development and change, and often those critical decisions to grow your team are made when things are at the breaking point. You just simply can't stretch yourself any further. The next thing you know you've got five or seven or ten employees that you now have to manage, as well as doing the technical work that you were doing before—whatever that work was. And then you need to make some additional capital investments to support those extra people. They all need a desk and a computer. You may have to buy another vehicle, upgrade the phone system, or even get a bigger office space.

The thing about this phase of your business journey is that it sneaks up on you. You're still being the professional that you once were, and at this stage there's no way that you are going to turn away potential work, because you still need to get those extra clients in. But now, you have to be the human relations manager, the administration manager, the finance manager, the marketing manager, and the operations manager as well. All of a sudden you find yourself having to deal with banking arrangements, finance agreements, building insurance policies, health and safety legislation, and a million other things.

And you still have to be a partner and a dad or mum as well. So while you may have a greater amount of cash coming in, if you really look closely, you might find that you are making less money than you were when it was just you, or just you and your partner. That time-flexibility thing hasn't worked out so well. And those nice clothes and designer handbags and first class business travel that you always dreamed of just seem to be further away than ever.

Seventy percent of businesses are stuck in what Daniel and Glen call the Struggle Zone. It's a bit like being on a treadmill. You're working as fast as you can but you just don't seem to make any progress. If, and only if, you either get very lucky or you do some serious work on your business, will you be able to pop out the top of that zone and into the next.

Daniel and Glen call this the Lifestyle Zone. Here, you've got some good contracts coming in, a steady stream of new leads, you've got a good and stable team behind you that you've recruited, you've put some good and robust business systems in place, and things are going pretty well. You have some free cash flow and your team can handle everything while you actually take a break and a well-deserved holiday. You might finally buy that designer handbag or speedboat that you've always wanted.

This has been my business journey. From solo-preneur, through struggle and into lifestyle, back to struggle, and back to lifestyle again. And this is a great time to point out that just because you get through one of these zones, it does not make you immune to regressing back to the same place later. Your business journey is not guaranteed to be linear.

Why am I telling you this? Having been an owner of a business in the Start-Up (solo-preneur) Zone, the Struggle Zone and the Lifestyle Zone, I can promise you that the last one is better. To quote the American actress Mae West, "I've been rich and I've been poor, and rich is better." My challenge to you is that your sole and overriding goal is to get out of the Struggle Zone.

My challenge to you is that your sole and overriding goal is to get out of the Struggle Zone.

That may mean that you consciously elect to stay as a solo-preneur. This can sound like heresy to some. Every business guru tells you to grow, grow, grow. However, I believe that it is a perfectly legitimate business decision for you as a business owner to remain as a solo-preneur and stay small. I know some solo-preneurs who are bringing in six or seven figures, so you don't need to feel guilty because you don't aspire to be the next Amazon, Google, or Apple.

Let's look at that 70%, the majority of businesses who are stuck in the Struggle Zone, and how they can get out of there. For most of these business owners, the number one success factor, the one big kicker to getting on the elevator to the Lifestyle Zone, is winning a contract with a large organisation.

For most small businesses, the spark for rapid business growth is winning a contract with a big organisation.

The Leap is Worthwhile, But Not Easy

I hope I have accurately painted the picture for you of what your business *can* look like once you step up into the Lifestyle Zone. Sounds attractive, doesn't it? There are definitely rewards to be had, but almost always, every aspect of your business will have to change and adapt—perhaps significantly. The range of outcomes will be somewhere between unsettled through to traumatised. Unfortunately business failure is too common. Be prepared to do some hard work on your business.

Having a big customer can be very rewarding, but if it were easy, everyone would be doing it.

So, if you are seeking a laid-back lifestyle, you are looking in the wrong place. Big companies can be very demanding, to the point of driving you to distraction. You will experience frustration to the point where you think you really will go mad, and wonder why on earth you ever decided to do this in the first place.

In the course of writing this book, I interviewed many small business owners who were already a supplier to a big organisation. Without exception, the interview inevitably went to a discussion of dealing with dumb decisions, bad management, over-the-top requirements, plan changes, and an endless supply of stories about delays and frustrations.

So, before you read any further in this book, please get yourself a pen and paper, a coffee, beer or glass of wine, and work through exactly why you want to go on this journey.

- Do you want to grow your business?
- How tolerant are you to the risk of business ups and downs?
- Do you know whether your product or service is actually required by big organisations?
- Are you prepared to commit considerable resources to make this happen?
- If you take on a big contract, will it benefit your family and life?
- If you start supplying to a big company, will it help to develop your products and services?
- Do you want to improve your business systems?
- Are you prepared to have your customers setting requirements in your workplace and sometimes enforcing apparently intrusive audits and assessments of your capabilities?
- Are you prepared to let other people play a management role in the business as it grows?
- Are you prepared to be frustrated beyond belief at times with requests and delays?
- Are you prepared to put your company at risk of having a contract pulled with zero notice?
- Do you have a "safety net" if you lose the business with your big customer? Does your company have adequate resilience?
- Do you have an exit plan once you have achieved your business goals?

You can also head to page 281 and locate the download option for this exercise as a worksheet worth working through.

If you have made it this far and have still decided that you want to go on, I hope I can help to prepare you for what is ahead.

Chapter 10
The Rewards to Be Enjoyed

I said at the end of the last chapter that you would have to make big changes in your business if you want to go on this path of attracting a big name as a customer, and I invited you to answer a few questions. For some business owners, the choice is to stay out of this space, and this is a perfectly legitimate choice.

For those who choose to forge on, there are real benefits to be gained.

Enhanced Credibility

If you make the commitment and get yourself ready to take on these contracts, you will open up a whole new range of business opportunities for yourself, and your business will move to a higher level. Everything you have put in place to meet the requirements for your first contract will assist you to also bid on local, state, and federal government contracts, and engage with any large business anywhere in the world. Landing that first big contract will give you the credibility to bid on the next, larger piece of work.

I have seen this happen time and time again over my business career; a small company solves a problem for a big customer and gets a one-off contract to perform a task. If they do that job well, they are then invited to put together a proposal for a slightly bigger task. Often, these smaller, initial tasks fly "under the radar". They are not valuable or critical enough to trigger a full-blown proposal or tender process, but they perform the very important function of building credibility. Prove your worth with that initial job, make your company contact look good or take a pain away for them, and before you know it, you're on "the list" and being invited to tender for more and more work.

Increased Revenue

Of course, the big attraction of getting work with big organisations is the revenue to be gained. Getting a multi-year contract to supply goods or services is gold for a small business owner. Turnover can be increased rapidly by gaining just one customer, instead of having to locate and convert multiple smaller customers—and then service them all individually. It is not unusual to see a small business take a 10-times leap in revenue by landing just one contract with a big company.

Improved Profitability

You will also find that by improving all your processes to the standard required to win work in a big company's supply chain, you will reap efficiencies within your organisation. You will find better ways of doing work you have always done in a faster time, using less resources, and thus improve your business profitability.

Certainty

The other side of the revenue coin is predictability. All of a sudden, your business has recurring and certain income, and the lumpy income of living from job to job is a thing of the past. Having been in that situation several times myself over my business career, I know just how distressing (and indeed debilitating) this can be. It's the 2 a.m. sweats, when you wake up wondering where the next bit of income is going to come from, and it all just seems impossible. Having the certainty of a fixed amount of revenue landing in the bank account every month is a beautiful thing for any small business owner.

The predictable revenue stream also gives you the latitude to make some long-term decisions that you would otherwise hesitate over. A common one is hiring more team members. There may be some additional expertise that would really add to your team, but taking them on with an uncertain future income is just a bridge too far. Having a contracted income for the foreseeable future can be the trigger for that decision.

Longevity

I know I said earlier that remaining as a solo-preneur is a perfectly legitimate business decision—and it is. However, we do know that the largest number of business start-ups and business exits are for businesses without employees—the solo-preneurs. The chances of a small business surviving really does increase with the number of employees. The relationship between business survival and number of employees is a complex one, but the bottom line is that taking a contract with a large organisation, and having more employees to service that contract, increases your chances of surviving and becoming a long-term success.

Chapter 11
Reasons Not to Do This

I've just spent an entire chapter telling you the upside of having a contract with a big buyer. But, of course, there is a downside as well. Let's look at some of the pitfalls to watch out for. I will give more detail on these in later chapters of the book, but what I'm trying to do here is just give you an overall picture.

Portfolio Risk

This is the "don't put all your eggs in one basket" lesson. I saw this happen so many times during the resources boom that we experienced in Australia from 2005 to 2012. Many small businesses were started on the promise of a contract from one of the big firms in the industry. Often, the person starting the new business had already been working for the company and was offered the chance to go out on their own, doing exactly the same work that they had been doing as an employee. As a result, the small business had only one customer. Often, the amount of work involved in that contract was all that the business could reasonably take on.

In other cases the small business is effectively barred from taking on contracts with another customer. Whatever the cause, the effect is that the small business is now a one-trick pony and totally vulnerable to a change of policy by the big customer. And of course, that is exactly what happened to many of them once the mining boom turned into a mining bust—their one customer disappeared and so did their business.

Effectively, **what the large company is doing is outsourcing their economic risk**. It is much easier to cut costs by eliminating supply contracts than to lay off thousands of workers once the bad times hit.

Cost Pressure

In times of economic stress, when large companies look to cut their costs, small suppliers are usually in the first line of cost-cutting. Contract administration is a real cost consideration for large companies, and reducing the number of contractors in a downturn is an easy way to cut costs. In tough times, one of the things that big buyers do is to move decision-making responsibility a few steps up the corporate ladder. For example, when the coal industry collapsed, site people we dealt with who formerly had a spend limit of $40,000 had their spending authority removed altogether. All spending decisions moved up at least two layers. What that effectively does is reduce decision making altogether. The painful process of sending requests upwards, waiting for approval and then a response meant that decisions weren't made at all. Small, local companies found that purchase orders were being cancelled or just not being issued at all, and their work dried up completely.

Time to Success

Landing a contract with a big buyer is not something that happens overnight. You will have heard sportsmen and women say something like, "It took me 12 years of hard work to become an overnight success." Hopefully it won't take you 12 years, but unless you are extraordinarily lucky, there is a lot of groundwork to do. The next chapter in this book will help you to do what is necessary, and set the foundations for a successful and continuing relationship with your new big customer.

Business Ethics and the Imbalance of Power

In a perfect world, everyone would be honourable, and business ethics lapses would be non-existent. Unfortunately though, the world is far from perfect, and not every person you deal with at your big company will treat your relationship as one seeking mutual benefit. I have seen (and been the subject of) corporate behaviour that takes advantage of the difference in power between a small and a large business.

Recently, the Australian Government has passed legislation that makes certain unfair contract terms illegal, in response to the prevalence of these clauses in "take it or leave it" contracts.

I hasten to add that not all your potential big customers are like this. There are hundreds of good firms out there with a much more mature approach to procurement—they realise that building a sustainable supply chain is a long-term game, and that success is a team sport. Your job as a business owner is to understand the type of beast you are dealing with, or trying to deal with, and be prepared.

Financial Risk

Once you have started your contract with your new, big customer, you are going to be dealing with larger amounts of money than you have previously. You may have to hold more stock, employ more people, or buy new equipment. All this costs money, and your working capital will have to be increased. You will have to make friends with your bank manager, and if you don't have sufficient funds in reserve, arrange a loan or a finance facility.

Then there is the issue of getting paid. It is well established that big companies are the worst at paying their bills late, particularly in Australia. A comprehensive inquiry in Australia found that the **worst payers are large and multinational businesses—and that they're getting worse.**[18] More than half the people who answered the inquiry's survey said that these companies were always or frequently late with their payments. Government departments and agencies also got a (dis)honourable mention. One in five small businesses reported that they were always or frequently late.

In the words of one of the respondents to the inquiry, "*We put due dates on our invoices and to some extent I see no point on putting a due date on as nobody ever looks at it, they pay when they feel ready.*"

Since the report of this inquiry was published in 2017, the Federal Government has introduced legislation that requires all companies with a turnover of greater than $100 million to report on their payment performance. The way that the reports are structured means we can't see how many invoices were paid after their actual due date. However, if we make the very reasonable assumption that anything over 30 days is "late", just over one third of invoices are still being paid late. Even if the trading terms are longer than 30 days, they shouldn't be.

You will also have to get used to extended payment terms, where the big company unilaterally imposes a 60, 90, or even 120 day payment period. You will be waiting longer for your cash, so again, you will have to have a good relationship with your bank manager to ensure you don't fall into a cash flow crisis.

---

18 Australian Small Business and Family Enterprise Ombudsman, *Payment Times and Practices Inquiry – Final Report*, April 2017, https://www.asbfeo.gov.au/sites/default/files/2021-11/ASBFEO_Payment_Times_and_Practices%20Inquiry_Report.pdf.

SECTION 3
SET YOUR FOUNDATIONS

By now, you will have made up your mind about whether you want to continue this journey of pursuing a big customer or not. If so, let's continue with some of the business basics that you must have in place before you start on the path to rapid growth. Just as you can't build a house on wobbly foundations, you can't build a business without establishing a stable base to build from.

In Section 2, we looked at the concept of the business journey. The object of this section is to help you build a solid foundation that will be a launch pad for your business so you can traverse the Struggle Zone as rapidly as possible.

Chapter 12
The Nine Essential Business Skills

Following the 2012 resources bust in Australia, I was part of a highly motivated group of people who banded together to see how we could help small businesses build the strength and resilience to withstand the economic upheavals that beset regional economies. Being part of that group made me think very deeply about exactly what is needed by a small business owner to create and sustain a thriving business.

In the end we decided on a list of nine core business skills:
- business/strategic planning
- financial management
- sales and marketing management
- operations management
- IT/digital capability
- human resource management
- procurement/supply chain management
- R&D, product or service development/innovation
- leadership development

That seems like a long and daunting list—especially for someone who has excellent technical skills but little in the way of business training, but wants to set up their own company. And it certainly is overwhelming. After more than 25 years in business, I am still learning and trying to be a better business owner every single day.

The critical thing to understand, however, is that while all these skills are necessary, not every business owner will need to be an expert in every skill. The idea of you being an expert of equal value across all parts of your business is extreme. Figure out what is needed in your type of business then work to your strengths, focus on what you do best, and bring in others as needed.

Michael Gerber's classic business book for small business operators describes it very well. In *The E-Myth Revisited*, Gerber describes three typical parts of a business person's ability as being the Manager, the Entrepreneur, or the Technician.

The Manager is someone who is good at managing the processes, the Entrepreneur is the visionary, and the Technician is great at "doing or creating the product or service". You might be one or two of these, but very unlikely to have equal strengths as all three. Understanding this can create a fundamental shift in how you view your own role in your business.

In addition to this, **all businesses are not the same**. There will be differences between a B2C (business-to-consumer) and a B2B (business-to-business) company. There will also be differences in the skills required according to the stage of your business journey. As your business grows, a higher level of any particular skill will probably be required.

While I am predominantly directing the information in this book at B2B business owners, never forget that all business is H2H (human-to-human) in the end.

You most probably started your business with a very basic (or even non-existent) business plan. There is absolutely nothing stopping you from registering a business name, hanging out your shingle, and starting to trade. But as your business grows and your turnover increases, the complexity of your business can expand, at times quite rapidly. At some point you are going to have to invest in some form of business planning for your company's future. Then your business planning efforts will have to step up yet another notch. You will be looking at long-term diversification strategies, succession planning, and exit planning. The same principle applies to the other eight business skills.

Therefore, the good news is that as a business owner, **you don't have to learn and do everything at once**. That insight allowed me to map out a continuous learning path—a business map if you like—to take away the feeling of overwhelm and let a business owner build their skills in an orderly fashion, consistent with the growth of their business.

You don't have to learn and do everything at once.

This book is not a management textbook, however, so I have no intention of writing a chapter on each of these business skills. Rather, I will point out some of the foundation skills and concepts you must have in place before you set out to capture your first big customer.

Chapter 13
What Business Are You In?

I ask this question whenever I present workshops to small business owners. All sorts of answers come flying back at me, including, "We'd do anything, anytime. Like the Goodies!"[19]

As a small business, that's not a good plan. In fact, as a big business, it's not a good plan either. This particular question has been the subject of several forests' worth of management textbooks, journal articles, research reports, and now a few squillion pages on the internet. But it still needs to be asked. Now, more than ever, business owners need to be very clear on what business they are in, and understand *that* business extremely well.

The classic example given in most textbooks is that of the railroads. Railway companies used to be a licence to print money. Growing economies needed them and the barriers to entry were very high, so competition was low. Railways were the place to be. Then commercial aeroplane flights became a reality, as well as cars and

---

19 *The Goodies* was a 1970s British television comedy show whose theme song included the lyrics, "We can take on any old line, anything, anytime …"

trucks. Suddenly, people were fulfilling their transport and freight needs by using planes, cars, and trucks. The railway companies tried to fight back, believing that they needed to defend their share of the transport market. And that was their mistake. They looked upon themselves as *railway* companies, not *transport* companies. What the customers needed was transport, not a train.

Economic history is littered with dead companies that failed to think deeply about this question. Remember Kodak, the company that made photographic film? Founded in 1888, Kodak eventually filed for Chapter 11 bankruptcy protection in 2012. The company retained its identity as a maker of photographic film, and failed to react to the challenge of digital photography. If the company directors had considered themselves to be in, say, the market of creating visual memories, Kodak might still be around today.

You, as a small business owner, must take responsibility for deciding what business you are in, and adapting to changes that are happening around you.

Are you a restaurant or a company who feeds people? During the 2020–2022 era of the global COVID-19 pandemic, many companies successfully asked this question and then pivoted to deliver on what they were really selling. Cafés and restaurants were excellent examples of this. Some eateries expanded their take-away options of pre-cooked meals; others packaged up DIY meals with ingredients and instructions on how to prepare them. People who would otherwise have been customers coming in with friends for dinner could experience their favourite (or new) dishes at home. This is a process of self-evaluation. Is what your customers really want to buy the same as what you think you are selling?

Are hairdressers selling haircuts or compliments? Are travel companies selling flights or happy family times? Are restaurants selling a meal or relationship-building experiences around a laden table?

Once you have decided what business you are in, your next challenge is to claim your special part of that market—your niche. The business owner I referred to earlier who was channelling *The Goodies* had certainly not thought about his niche, but the business owner in my next case study certainly has.

> **In the real world ...**
> *The food industry must be one of the most competitive industries to enter. How many coffee shops, cafés, and small restaurants are there in your area? It must be difficult to identify and claim a niche, but there is a café owner in Brisbane, Australia who has nailed it. The Jam Pantry uses only produce sourced directly from farmers for its menu items and the wonderful jams, relishes, and chutneys they make and sell. While that in itself is great, they have gone one step further. Many city residents have their own veggie garden, but often grow more than they can eat. Pumpkins are easy to grow, but there's only so many you can eat yourself. These growers can bring their excess home-grown produce to the café, and exchange it for some of those wonderful preserves made from someone else's produce. This very narrow niche is obviously working—you have to book a long time ahead to get a table.*

Chapter 14
What's Your Purpose?

The next question is: **why do you do what you do?** This may sound like a very simple question, and the temptation is to give a very simple answer—like, "To make a profit." But you need to dig a bit deeper than that.

Why do you get up in the morning? Why do you do what you do? Why did you start your business? What drives you to keep going when things are tough? One particularly good question to ask yourself is this question that one of my business mentors uses when helping others to find their purpose: "*What do you rave on about after you've had couple of red wines or beers?*"

Here are a few other prompts to help you:
- What is it that gets you fired up when you start talking to your mates?
- What is it that you could stand up and talk passionately about for 10 minutes to an audience without much preparation? No notes, no palm cards, and no prompts on your iPad?
- What is it that is inside you that you need (not just want) to get out and share with the world?

Because that is your deep and enduring purpose.

Why Is It Important to Know Your Purpose?

For each of us there is something that we really do care about, and your customers will be able to detect that. Simon Sinek, a renowned leadership expert and author of the book *Start With Why*, puts it this way: *"People don't buy what you do; they buy why you do it."*

I like to answer the question of why it's important to know your purpose by asking a few more questions.

Question 1: What outcomes do you want for your business? Presumably, your answer will include things such as:
- growth
- profit
- be the business that others refer customers to
- social licence
- resilience
- longevity
- impact

Question 2: Who do you need to achieve these positive outcomes for your business? Again, I'm confident that your answers will look like the list below:
- employees
- customers
- suppliers
- shareholders
- financiers

Question 3: What do these people need in order to be persuaded to do business with you? There's a one-word answer—***trust***. To get these people and organisations to help you effectively, you need them to trust you.

The challenge with trust is that it takes time and effort to build. You can't buy it or impose it on others. They have to come to believe your organisation is trustworthy by themselves, and be convinced by your actions.

Trust is like putting money in the bank. Every "transaction" you have with your customers, suppliers, shareholders, etc., is an opportunity to put a bit of trust into your "trust bank". If you abuse that trust, though, those deposits can be withdrawn immediately and permanently.

Question 4: Why would those people trust you? What builds up their trust in you sufficiently that they will engage with you?

The answer? Your ***actions***—the things you do, the way your business behaves and presents itself to the world. They will see your marketing, how you treat your employees, whether you contribute to your community, your truthfulness …

Now we come to the last question.

Question 5: What drives your company's actions?

What makes everybody in your organisation do the things they do. What drives your vision, mission, ESG performance,[20] etc. What underpins and drives your company's values?

It is your organisation's **purpose**—the reason your organisation exists. I like this definition:

An organisation's purpose is its meaningful and enduring reason to exist, that aligns with long-term financial performance, provides a clear context for daily decision making, and unifies and motivates relevant stakeholders.

---

20 ESG performance is how well a company meets particular sustainability metrics specifically relating to environmental, social, or governance issues.

Purpose-led companies show, on a daily basis, that they are worthy of high levels of trust, and they are rewarded accordingly.

Your employees care

Purpose-led companies become an "employer of choice" and can recruit and retain the best candidates. Employees who understand and share the owner's motivation will themselves be motivated to perform. If your purpose is shining like a beacon, clearly guiding your actions, and making you an enthusiastic leader, it's very hard for others to not want a piece of what it is you're having.

Purpose-led companies experience 50% less staff turnover, 13% higher productivity, and overall increased employee morale.

Your purpose guides your decision-making process

There will inevitably be times when you are tested in your business and have to make difficult decisions. Being crystal clear on your purpose will remind you of your values and help you make the right decision for your business. Your purpose gives you a reason to carry on.

You probably already know that running a small business inevitably involves some tough times, when you seem to be working so hard but getting nowhere. Having a driving purpose gives you a sense of direction which in turn will give you the strength and reason to put one foot after another, and carry on.

Chapter 15
What's in Your PESTLE Environment?

The next business skill you need to acquire is being hyper-aware of your business environment. What is happening outside your organisation that could affect how you operate? To ensure that you don't overlook any possible influencing factors, somebody clever came up with the acronym PESTLE:

- P—political
- E—economic
- S—social
- T—technological
- L—legal
- E—environmental

I have included some examples in the table below to get you started on scanning your own business environment.

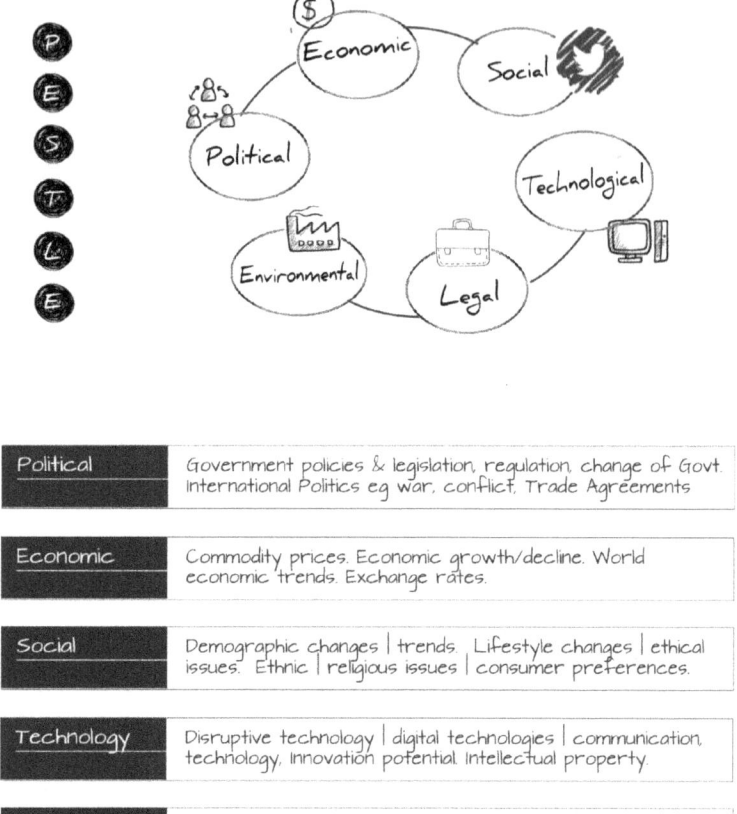

Political	Government policies & legislation, regulation, change of Govt. International Politics eg war, conflict, Trade Agreements
Economic	Commodity prices. Economic growth/decline. World economic trends. Exchange rates.
Social	Demographic changes	trends. Lifestyle changes	ethical issues. Ethnic	religious issues	consumer preferences.
Technology	Disruptive technology	digital technologies	communication technology, Innovation potential Intellectual property.
Legal	Employment law. Health and Safety law. Discrimination law. Company law. Laws on business structures. Taxation law.
Environmental	Global warming. Natural disasters. Your impact on the environment Community expectations.

Undertaking a PESTLE analysis is an excellent opportunity to involve your team in the business planning process. By involving all disciplines and levels of your company, you will be much more able to identify all the possible outside influences that may impact you, and build up a much clearer picture of the challenges and opportunities faced by your business.

You can access a PESTLE worksheet to use in your next planning session with your team at the back of this book or via my website. It's yours to use and share, with my compliments.

Chapter 16
Who Is Your Ideal Customer?

Who are you going to sell your products and services to? Hint: the answer is not "anyone" or "everyone". In the same way that you need to spend some time considering what business you are really in, you also need to think very clearly and closely about who your ideal customer is. Without truly understanding who your customer is and what they want, how can you produce a product or service that really meets their needs?

I know that this book is about attracting and working with big organisations. So, your reply to the question above may be "the federal government" or "a large supermarket chain". Yes, that is partially correct, but there is a person within that organisation who is going to make that fateful decision—to give you a contract or not. Marketing gurus speak of creating a customer "avatar", a representation of your ideal customer.

Here are some questions you can use with your team to help you create your customer avatar:
- Are they male or female?

- Where do they live?
- How old are they?
- What level of education have they reached?
- Do they have children? How many?
- What magazines do they read?
- What TV programs do they watch?
- What social media sites do they use?
- What does their work day look like?
- When and why do they buy your product/service?
- What does your product/service make them feel like?

What Does Your Customer Really Want?

This is another seemingly simple question, but you have probably detected a pattern by now and may sense that this question also needs more thought.

If you are selling tyres and tyre fitting (a product and a service) it would be easy to say, "My customer ran over a nail so she needs a new tyre." And that would be perfectly true, but that thinking does not go far enough. Does the customer want a tyre, or does she need the ability to keep driving her car to get to work?

What she really wants is the benefit of having a fully inflated tyre on her car so she can drive it. Your business can provide her with a tyre and put it on her car, so what can you do with your product and service to meet her needs better than your competition? Perhaps "while you wait" tyre fitting, or the offer of a vehicle to drive while you fix the tyre? These alternatives would move closer to providing her with what she really wants—to be back on the road doing all the things that are necessary in her day.

The example above shows how understanding what your customer really wants can help you to create products and services that give them a reason to buy from you, and only you. Marketing people call this your *unique selling proposition*, or USP.

Having established your customer avatar, you can now do some in-depth thinking about what your customers' problems are, and how you can help to fix them. Are they trying for a promotion at work? Are they overloaded with work that you could help them with? Are they under budget pressure from their supervisor?

You need to understand the total value of your product or service from your customers' point of view.

Understanding what your customer needs really is the key to selling anything. Take the example of luxury goods. Why would anyone spend $5,000 or even $50,000 on a watch? A smart phone or a $10 watch from the markets will tell you the time, and surely that's all an expensive watch will do. Expensive handbags also fall into the same category. If you need a handbag to carry things in, why not use a plastic bag from the supermarket? My current handbag is one of those hessian shopping bags from a major supermarket. It's perfectly serviceable! The reason is that people purchase these goods for a feeling of emotional wellbeing, not because they need to tell the time or carry their money. It may be to reward ourselves—for a promotion, for example—or to gain acceptance from others, or simply just to show off.

What's Your Value Proposition?

Having established what your customer actually wants, you can now craft your *value proposition*—what it is that is going to attract your ideal client to your company and not your competitor. Your written value proposition will tell your potential customers what value (specific benefits) you will bring, how you will solve their problem, and what your unique selling proposition is.

Before you go any further, please check these points:
- I know my ideal customer.

- I know who they are.
- I know where to find them.
- I know what they are seeking to solve a problem or challenge.
- I know the problems and challenges they face.
- I understand what they appreciate the most about my products or services.
- I have a unique value proposition that suits my ideal customer.
- I know WHY I do this.
- My employees also know these things.

Chapter 17
You Have to Pay the Admission Price

I know that your parents probably told you that nothing good comes without hard work. In business that's also true. But hard work isn't enough—it's got to be *smart* work as well.

If you want to reap the rewards of having a big company as a customer, you're going to have to do some up-front work. In other words, if you want to play a bigger game, you're going to have to be prepared to pay the price of admission to the better seats at the game.

For the small business owner, this starts with research—research about your prospect. If you are already in the industry where your target is positioned, chances are that you are already quite knowledgeable about that industry, and are aware of its idiosyncrasies. But that isn't enough. You need to know about *your* prospect in particular. Remember, your targets are extremely busy people. If you finally manage to score a face-to-face meeting, nothing will kill the buzz like you saying, "Now, tell me about your company." Luckily for you, this technology-enabled age has made this task so much easier.

You can find out a treasure trove of information from social media sites such as LinkedIn or Quora.

Here are six core questions about the company you need to know the answers to:
1. Who works at the company?
2. Who fills the decision-making positions?
3. Who are the main players connected to?
4. What groups do they belong to?
5. What do they post about on LinkedIn?
6. What are the main problems they talk about?

If you would like to download a checklist for this, you'll find a link to one on page 281.

I recommend you create a fresh sheet for each company you wish to research, and work through these questions thoroughly.

As part of your research, you'll also want to follow financial and/or industry news for media releases about company activities and significant events.

Here are six core questions about news and opportunities you need to know the answers to:
1. Are they releasing a new product?
2. Have they taken over another company?
3. Are they launching into a new strategic direction?
4. Are there any government decisions that will affect them?
5. Do any company changes create an opportunity for you to approach them with your solution?
6. Do you know anyone who already works in that company who might also be worth connecting with?

Your competitors can also be a source of valuable information. Check their website for any research studies or case studies that will give you a clue as to the problems they are solving for your prospect.

Chapter 18
Understanding Portfolio Risk—Having All Your Eggs in One Basket

The thought of having just one large customer to serve is certainly enticing. Here are some of the great reasons for having just one key client to work with:
- Your administration would be so much simpler.
- Your team members could become super-skilled in your customer's product.
- Their money arrives in your bank account month in, month out.
- No more incessantly chasing up new business leads.
- *What could possibly go wrong?*

Then one day the phone call arrives. "We've decided that we are not going to progress that project," or "We've decided to change suppliers."

At this point, you have that sinking, sick feeling in your

stomach. You've already resourced this project, employed people with the required skills, purchased equipment ... Somewhere along the line, your company became a one-trick pony, and the consequence has been revealed in all its horror. You are now faced with some awful decisions.

This is exactly what happened to our environmental consultancy company, and thousands of others, as the mining boom came to an end. The beginnings of our company were in agribusiness, but in the mid-2000s, the mining industry started to take off as Chinese demand for Australia's mineral commodities boomed. We started off with one small contract with a mining giant that didn't even involve us having to be on a mine site. We performed that contract well and were invited to put forward a proposal to do more work—this time on the mine site. Again, we performed our tasks well, and gradually the amount of work from this one client was making up more than 60% of our turnover. The upside was that we were acquiring new skills that, in turn, allowed us to bid for other contracts. Of course, there was also the certainty of that monthly cash flow. The downside, however, was that we recognised we were extremely vulnerable should something go wrong with that contract.[21]

Using our new skill sets, we set about diversifying away from the mining industry (and agribusiness) into the oil and gas industry. We did that so successfully, in fact, that one gas company quickly took top spot on our client list and was providing more than 60% of our revenue. We did our best during this period to maintain a balance across sectors, but the resources industry had taken over the regional economy to such an extent that trying to balance resources work against agribusiness, industrial, and government work was impossible. However, the percentage of business from our top one and top three customers was one of our monthly metrics so we could

---

21 That didn't happen fortunately, and we were still undertaking that work some 15 years on when this second edition was being prepared for publication.

at least identify where the risk was coming from.

Then the downturn hit. In three months, we took six of those dreaded phone calls. Six projects that we had fully resourced with people and equipment were summarily cancelled. In that situation, it is extremely difficult to reduce costs as quickly as your revenue is declining. Wages are sticky, mining equipment was worth about as much as a Matchbox car to sell, and wholesale sacking of staff members is not something anyone wants to do—especially in a small business where team members become almost like family.

However, despite that very scary situation, we were in a much better position than many other small business owners who only had one contract with one company. I saw businesses that employed 40 or more people disappear overnight as their one contract was cancelled. Some of those were ex-employees who had been given the opportunity to start a business doing the same work they had been doing previously, as consultants and not employees, and as a result they had limited business skills. Others survived but were mortally wounded—in some cases they were offered continuation of their contract but at a greatly reduced rate. They struggled on for several years, only to succumb eventually. Others still managed to stay afloat but carried a huge load of debt and the accompanying stress.

Of course, not every small business failed to survive the end of the resources boom. Many not only survived but thrived. In every case I know of, those companies had spread their business across several customers and/or industry sectors. They had a low **concentration ratio**.

Many small business books, accountants, and specialists recommend a regular check of your concentration ratio, and the **Pareto principle** is commonly referred to—the principle that 80% of consequences arise from only 20% of the causes. In this instance, 80% of your business might come from approximately 20% of your customers. The "80/20 rule" also acknowledges such things as 20%

of your services might generate 80% of your revenue. It's therefore worth doing this quick exercise on at least an annual basis. However, the concentration ratio is specifically about individual companies you supply to and the percentage of your turnover that comes from them.

Calculate Your Concentration Ratio

From your financial accounting system, find the customer that has given you the most revenue. You could do this on a monthly, quarterly, or annual basis. In our company, we measure and report this monthly. Then, find your gross revenue for the same period.

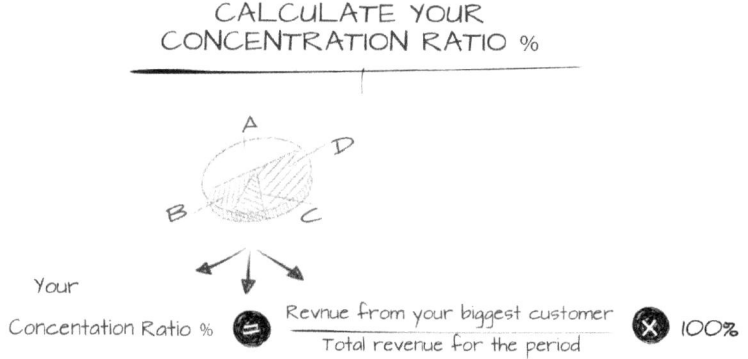

So what is the appropriate concentration ratio for a small business? This is a bit like asking how long a piece of string is. A quick internet search, including of academic research articles, easily turns up many different definitions. Recommendations range from 8% up to 20%, reflecting the fact that different ratios are appropriate for:
- The growth stage of your company. At the inception of your business, having just one customer may be a major milestone on your business journey.
- The size of your turnover. As your turnover grows, you should be looking to add more customers rather than just relying on your one foundation client.

- The niche you occupy. A general accountant could have hundreds of customers, whereas a provider of specialist forensic accountancy services has a much smaller group of potential customers.
- The industry you occupy. Some industries are much more prone to cyclical ups and downs than others. Agriculture, mining, and construction spring easily to mind, so concentration of your customers in that one industry is risky.

Apart from posing a real threat to your business growth, and even its very existence, customer concentration can kill your chances of a business exit. Potential buyers will be looking at the impact of losing at least one customer in the transition to new owners. Having a high customer concentration ratio is a sure-fire way to decrease your potential exit price.

Chapter 19
Your External Team

There is a plethora of information available on human resource management for small business owners. Recruiting, training, and keeping the best possible team—your internal team—is a critical success factor. But there is another team that I believe is equally as important, but receives much less attention—your ***external team***.

Being a small business owner is a team sport, and you need a professional team to support you.

At a minimum, you need:
- an accountant
- a banker
- a lawyer
- an insurance broker

My personal preference is for them all to have at least a bit of grey hair. You don't need to be someone's training ground or guinea pig. I know that everyone has to start their career somewhere, but it doesn't have to be on your account.

Your Accountant

I have seen far too many businesses do immense damage to themselves by trying to save money on their accountancy services. Do not use your brother-in-law's sister's cousin who does a few people's books from a table in the corner of her kitchen because she gives you "family rates". As always, you will get what you pay for—not much. The Australian Government has a habit of changing taxation laws every week—well, perhaps that's a little exaggeration, but sometimes it feels that way. Your accountant needs to be on top of all these changes and their implications for your business. To fall behind on your reporting and filing responsibilities can mean a slow "commercial death by taxes". Medium and large accounting firms spend a significant amount of time and money on professional development and education for a reason—so they can pass it on to their clients. That means you.

Your accountant needs to have a large and preferably varied client base. Ideally, they will be located in or draw a significant number of clients from your area—either geographical or industry. They will therefore be dealing with many businesses similar to yours, serving the same clients as you, and subject to similar market conditions as you. They can and should, therefore, be an invaluable source of market intelligence.

Your accountant should be able to answer these questions easily:
- What are other businesses experiencing?
- Is there a trend towards lengthening payment terms?
- What practices are being employed in tender allocations?
- What's happening to property values and rents in the area?
- Are the banks lending more or less to small business?

Your well-connected, up-to-date accountant will be all over this market intelligence, and will gladly pass it on to you freely. Well, it's not free, but it is part of what you'd be paying for anyway if your accountant had no local knowledge.

Changing accountants is not technically difficult. You will need to obtain an "ethical letter" from your new accountant of choice, requesting that your former accountant hand over all your files to your chosen new accountancy practice. But it can be hard where personal or long-standing relationships are involved. The ultimate question you must answer as a business owner is: what is more important? Your business (and the attached spouse, kids, employees, school fees, self-managed super fund, mortgage …), or your short-term discomfort and feeling bad about telling this person that they no longer serve the interests of your business?

Your Banker

You will have less control over your banker. The size of your bank account (read: "loans") will dictate the level at which you are allocated a banker by your bank of choice. You can be lucky, and be allocated a bright young banker on an upward trajectory. Or you can be unlucky, and be allocated one who has been sent to a regional branch prior to retirement. However, in Australia, you always have the option of changing banks altogether. Granted, changing banks is akin to getting a divorce but, like divorce, sometimes it has to be done in the interest of all concerned. And the major banks play on the fact that they have you roped and tied.

If you are using a reputable accounting firm, chances are that they will have as part of their team a finance specialist who can help you to review your loans and negotiate a better deal with a different bank or your existing bank. (This, of course, is another good reason to not use your brother-in-law's sister's cousin as your accountant.) It is not unusual for small business owners to save almost a full percentage point on loan interest rates by changing banks.

Your professional accountant will also have existing relationships with other professionals you may find yourself in need of at some stage. The most common of these is a legal advisor. The work of an accountant and a lawyer overlap in many areas, and having them both working together towards the same outcome is vital. For example, choosing a business structure is one of the most important foundation decisions you must make when you establish a business. Your accountant, together with a lawyer, will be able to advise you on the best structure for your situation, allowing you to avoid an expensive re-adjustment later on.

The face of business financing is also changing as millennial and gen Z business owners take over from their boomer elders. They are ambivalent about traditional banking. Gen Z SME owners are happy using fintech lenders and seeking venture capital, giving them much more flexibility in how they finance their businesses.

This is probably just as well, as the traditional primary source of finance for small businesses is all but closed to them—mortgaging the family home. If you can't afford to buy a home, you certainly can't use it as collateral. (It will be interesting to see how traditional banks adjust to this paradox).

While I have written about the importance of your banker as a part of your external team, the face of small business lending in Australia is rapidly changing. The big change for small business is the rise of so-called "fintech" lenders. These are non-bank organisations that are using technology to disrupt the finance industry. They provide loans to small businesses without the sacrifice of an average forest and an extended wait for each loan. Loans can be approved almost in real-time. Fintech lending grew from zero in 2014 to $25 million in 2015, to $3.6 billion in 2021 (down from $3.8 billion in 2019 due to business slow-down caused by the COVID-19 pandemic).[22]

How this new twist to small business lending will turn out, I

---

22   Australian Financial Review. (2022). *The $4 billion pay off: 850 fintechs powering Australia's digital finance sector*. [online] Available at: https://www.afr.com/technology/4-billion-powers-the-nation-s-fintech-sector-20220520-p5an2c

have no idea, but there is clearly a strong demand for this service by small business owners who feel they have been let down or ignored by the large banks.

In 2022, Australia had about 850 active fintechs, and the global consultancy firm EY estimates that the sector is earning about $4 billion in annual revenue. The entire banking and finance industry is undergoing a massive transformation. In December 2017, just two months after the first edition of this book was published, a Royal Commission was established to examine the practices of the Australian banking, finance and superannuation industries. Over the following two years, the commission uncovered a culture lacking in ethics, where money and profit overrode both the law and the bounds of human decency. Several recommendations from the commission have been implemented. However, I have no doubt that improvements in behaviour won't be permanent. Australia has a long tradition of Inquires into misdeeds in the financial system. Findings are made, we all gasp in horror (including the Government), the institutions blame a few bad apples, some laws are enacted, and in 10–20 years, we repeat the entire process.

Combine those changes with the rise of fintech (including buy now pay later companies, digital banks, and blockchain and cryptocurrency), and you have a moveable feast of innovation and change. I am optimistic that this changed banking/finance scene will be of benefit to SME owners and managers.

You will need to keep an eye on how this develops, as it may be a way to more easily access the finance that you need to grow your business.

Your Lawyer

Saving money by choosing a cheap lawyer is another faux pas committed by many a start-up. There is nothing quite as expensive as a cheap lawyer.

Choosing a lawyer or law firm is difficult. Here, you are probably looking less for local knowledge, and more for subject specialisation to do with your particular industry. As with an accountant, choosing a sole practitioner will probably not give you the breadth of experience and knowledge that will be necessary as your small business grows.

As soon as you start dealing with big companies or government you will find that they have tag-teams of lawyers, and you can be sure that they have been all over any documentation that they put in front of you. Think of your lawyer as an insurance policy. You take out insurance policies knowing that the cost of an annual insurance policy is a lot less that the cost of rebuilding your house and purchasing new contents should a fire strike. Once you have been sued, the cost of your lawyer will seem insignificantly small.

One of the main reasons you will be using your lawyer is for their advice on contracts. Contracts are such an important issue for small businesses that we have devoted one complete chapter to them in an attempt to point out some of the main pitfalls. I have seen contracts put in front of small business owners that are nothing short of unconscionable. and the Australian Government has finally taken action and made such conditions illegal (See Chapter 7).

The easiest solution is to establish a relationship with a major firm. This has two advantages. Firstly, a large firm will have access to specialists in almost any subject area you can think up. At a minimum, you are going to need legal advice on:

- Contracts
- Property sales and purchases
- Business Structures
- Intellectual Property
- Tax

And it is highly unlikely that a single small practitioner will have a suite of skills to cover all these areas.

Secondly, there is a significant amount of authority that goes with having the letterhead of a major national or international firm on documents representing your company. One multinational is more likely to take notice of another multinational than a solo practitioner.

The downside, of course, is that your national or international firm will cost a lot more, but peace of mind has to have a price tag. Try searching for the middle ground. There are some medium-sized law firms that house specialist skills, but don't carry quite the price tag that their national/international counterparts do. Talk to your accountant. Most accounting firms will have a trusted legal firm they work with.

Your Insurance Broker

Choosing an insurance broker can be a real trap for new business owners. I have already explained how much your potential big customers hate risk, so one of the first things they are going to ask you for is proof that you have the right insurance. This will include the following types of insurance:

- Public Liability
- Prfessional Indemnity
- Workers Compensation
- Plant and Equipment
- Vehicle

It is vital that your insurance broker really understands your business and the types of risk you face. At one stage, I had reason to investigate our professional indemnity (PI) insurance, having been offered the opportunity to obtain a quote from a different broker through a professional association. My investigations showed that our company was not even covered for one type of work we were doing regularly at the time.

Professional indemnity insurance will be the most expensive insurance you will have, and may also prove to be the hardest to obtain. However, in the majority of cases, you will not even get past first base doing work for a big company without it. If your company is a member of a professional association, ask them if there is a specialist PI insurance provider to your industry. A specialist provider will usually be able to provide comprehensive cover at a lower price.

An additional service to enquire about is whether your professional indemnity insurer will provide you with advice on contracts you have been asked to sign. Many PI insurers will offer a limited number of contract reviews as part of your PI insurance. This is an extremely valuable service. A contract review by your lawyer will probably cost in the vicinity of $600–$2,000, so you should make use of it to the maximum.

Your Business Mentor or Coach

A business coach or mentor is not a necessity in the same way that an accountant, financier, or lawyer are. However, just as top football teams full of excellent players who know how to play the game have coaches to help them to be their best, you probably should too, and be prepared to pay for one.

Having that person who stands outside your business but understands it well will be of enormous value as your business grows. But as with all the other professionals I have mentioned, getting a good one is the trick.

I make a distinction between a coach and a mentor.

Coaching is more structured, and usually intended to impart a specific set of skills. It is therefore often a shorter-term relationship, and sometimes delivered in a group setting. There are good coaches and not-so-good coaches. Some simply follow a manual, with little regard for the particular circumstances of the business, the owner or the industry. Then there are specialist coaches who have a deep, demonstrated skill set they have developed over their career, who will teach you those skills.

A mentor is someone who has significant experience, knowledge and expertise, and has the interpersonal skills to share them in a trusting environment. Mentoring has a significant development component for the mentee and their business, but may be more general and less structured than coaching. Your mentor will see the potential in you and want to see you succeed as a business owner and as a person. In essence, the mentor helps you become a better version of yourself over time, through the transfer of knowledge from one generation (the mentor) to another (the mentee).

It is possible to find both skills in one person, but such treasures are rare. I am very fortunate to have had some of these people in my life.

Whether you engage a coach, a mentor, or both, the best plan of attack is to ask for recommendations from people you know and trust—preferably in your own industry. Many people call themselves business coaches/mentors without any qualifications to do so. Consequently, there are lots of them offering very poor service at a premium price. You may have to try a couple until you find someone who really fits with you and your business.

Chapter 20
Financial Management— Getting Paid

It's crushing, I know. I've been there. You've finally landed a contract with a big name that you've been chasing for ages. You've outlaid a significant amount of cash to "gear up" and do the best possible job to impress your new customer, but now you can't get paid.

Every small business owner knows—or should know—that cash flow is vital. Failure to control cash flow, in its various guises, is the most common cause of small business failure. It is also one of the main causes of dysfunctional stress for the small business owner, with all the consequential health and life issues.

There is no shortage of advice for small business owners on how to collect their accounts payable. Just do a simple Google search and you will instantly come up with tens of thousands of articles to read.

But working with large organisations can be a bit different, and it's important for the small business owner to understand that.

Here are some things that you need to take into consideration when you are working for a large buyer, such as government, a big corporation, or even a not-for-profit organisation.

There Is a Special Place in Cyberspace …

It may even be a parallel universe, but it's where invoices sent to large, bureaucratic organisations go if the stars don't align when they reach the accounts payable department. Once they enter that black hole, it's extremely difficult to get them back, so it's best to get the process right so they don't go there in the first place.

Understand That You Are Dealing with a Bureaucracy, Not Your Contacts

Large companies and government departments can have tens or even hundreds of thousands of employees, sometimes spread over several continents. Your contact is just one of them, and regardless of the strength and longevity of your relationship, they are a part of that bureaucracy. The only way to control an organisation of that size is as a bureaucracy—with all the built-in controls, fail-safe procedures, and processes, all designed to reduce risk. These controls are especially evident when it comes to them handing over money—i.e., paying your invoices.

Don't Work Without a Purchase Order

Critical point #1: Don't work without a contract, and don't do any work without a supporting purchase order or written confirmation. Ever.

Critical point #2: You must have some form of confirmation that will clearly demonstrate that you have been cleared to work by *someone with sufficient authority.*

No matter how much pressure you come under from your contacts within the organisation, resist, and read points #1 and #2 again. If you stray outside the boundaries, you drastically reduce your chances of getting paid for the work you perform—by about 100%. Below is an extract from a large company's recent email to all its suppliers that clearly illustrates the point:

*No goods or services are to be delivered to or at **any** XYZ Company location unless vendors have received a valid XYZ Company purchase order. If work is completed without a valid purchase order it could result in no payment.*

There will be no guarantee of payment if work is not approved by the relevant personnel. Even if approved after the work is completed, the payment process will be significantly delayed.

Get the Details Right

Large organisations have a multitude of departments, subsidiary companies, joint ventures and so on. It is important to have the invoicing details absolutely correct; including:
- the name of the entity
- the company or tax number (or whatever is needed to make the invoice legal in your jurisdiction)
- the contract, purchase order number, etc.

I always advise a meeting, phone call, or email with a contact person at the beginning of the engagement to ensure this is all made clear. Some large companies and governments even put this information on their website for suppliers to access easily. This is a very common cause of delayed invoice payments, as they have to be sent back for re-issue and approval.

Get the Format Right

As well as checking the invoicing details, make sure you check the format of the invoice before you start. Some organisations require line items, itemised in painstaking detail. Others just want a single line with a description like "Services provided for the month of January", or simply referring to a PO, contract, or proposal document.

Check the Payment Time

Usually, contracts with a large organisation will come with standard and non-negotiable payment terms. Make sure you are fully aware of these and take them into consideration when planning your cash flow. Payment terms of 60 days are typical, and 120 days is not unusual. Another common term is payment X days from the end of the month when the invoice is received, and this can create a significant time lag. The effect of this can be seen from the table below:

Fill in date for :	Dated	No. of days after work done	No. of days since Invoice Issued
Work Completed	04|12|2015		
Invoice Issued	04|01|2016	31	
Invoice Due	16|03|2016	103	72

In this case, if you had paid some costs associated with the original work performed, you will be out of pocket for 103 days. At best, you would be waiting 72 days to get your money. Your employees won't wait that long, and most of your suppliers probably won't either.

Australian businesses are known for being late payers. The average number of days late varies over the years, heavily influenced by economic conditions. As at the middle of 2021, the average late payment days across all Australian industries was just over 11 days.

However, there is a constant feature – big companies are the worst offenders.[23] These are exactly the organisations that you are targeting, so you must be prepared. Recommendations have been made to the Australian Government to legislate maximum payment terms for all business-to-business transactions. I would certainly vote for that piece of legislation.

Invoice Immediately

The graphic in the previous point clearly shows the importance of getting your invoices out as soon as possible. This is the real stumbling block for many small business owners—they love doing the work, but hate the "paperwork stuff". Just remember that when you went into business, your plan was to do good work that you love, that provides value and solves a problem for your customer. You didn't set out to be a banker to a multinational company or a government. Get your money, and let someone else provide them with credit.

By not sending your invoices out immediately, you aren't just hurting your own cash flow. You will be annoying your valuable big customer. You would think that they would be happy to have your invoice late, but that's actually not the case. I don't want to make this chapter an accounting lesson, but I'll try to explain why. It all comes down to a thing called ***accruals***.

Many small businesses think in terms of cash accounting. Cash comes in when it comes in, and goes out when it goes out. Simple. Large organisations, however, use ***accrual accounting***. As best they can, they try to make sure that their financial statements for any time period contain the revenue that was earned (rather than actually received), along with the expenses incurred to make that

---

23 DAngola, M. (2021). *Construction, retail and transport sectors struggle to pay bills.* [online] illion. Available at: https://www.illion.com.au/construction-retail-and-transport-sectors-struggle-to-pay-bills/.

revenue, even if they haven't been actually paid for. This way they have a more accurate picture of what they have earned and what it has cost them to earn it.

So, if the big company has some work done by your business in June, but doesn't get the invoice until July, the company needs to "accrue" for that amount. Even though the invoice wasn't paid, the cost of that work is in the books for June. Unlike cash accounting, keeping accrual financial records takes quite a bit of work, and there are entire departments of people whose job it is to make sure all these records are accurate. When you don't submit your invoice for months after the work is done, your delay plays havoc with the company's financial statements when the amounts owed have not been accrued for.

Check the Payment Terms

Check all the other terms associated with getting your invoices paid. Another common term is payment X days from approval of invoice. Generally, once your invoice has been received by accounts payable, it will be sent to the person responsible for your contract for approval. If that person is away for some reason, or simply neglects dealing with it (yes, it does happen—a lot), your invoice can languish in limbo for some time. The countdown for payment doesn't start until the invoice has been dealt with and approved. This is a very good reason to make sure the invoice is 100% correct when it leaves your office.

Copy in Your Contact When You Send the Invoice

Always cc the person who is going to be responsible for approving your invoice when you send it to accounts payable. That way, any issues they pick up can be dealt with quickly, the invoice re-issued if necessary, and the payment process will stay on track.

Phone a Friend

As I explained earlier in this chapter, there is a black hole where the invoices that don't conform to requirements go. Often, the accounts payable process has been outsourced—maybe to another continent. You need an ally within the organisation who can navigate the labyrinth of the accounts payable process. Make a point of identifying and befriending this person early, before you have to call on them. While this may seem to be a pain, and in an ideal world wouldn't be necessary, your initial effort will be repaid many times over if you actually find yourself in the situation of chasing a payment that nobody will take responsibility for.

Of course, there is much more to getting paid than just these points, but when you're dealing with a big customer that has a bureaucracy to navigate, these are a very good start. That way, you can reap all the advantages of having a big "name" as one of your customers.

Chapter 21
Growth, Downsizing, and Exit Strategies

Almost every management book or course that you encounter will have loads of information about how to manage growth in your business, as will later sections of this book. However, as I mentioned earlier in this section, there are certain industries that are particularly susceptible to large swings in demand and confidence. The resources industry is notoriously cyclical swinging from extremely high highs to extremely low lows. The building and construction industry is another that experiences booms and busts.

As of the first quarter of 2017, Australia had experienced 25 years without an economic recession, so this country had an entire generation of business owners who had known nothing other than buoyant trading conditions. In 2020, the world experienced a huge shock as the reality of the global COVID-19 pandemic hit us all. Effectively, the world ground to a halt for a time, with catastrophic consequences for many businesses, their owners and families, communities and national economies. Australia experienced its first recession since 1991 and many business owners did not have a plan for a financial downturn – let alone one with the severity of a global pandemic.

Governments regularly interfere in the economy, creating artificial demand or supply conditions in a particular industry. An excellent example was the Australian Home Insulation Program which was launched in 2009, where homeowners were compensated for installing insulation in their ceilings as an environmental protection measure. The massive, sudden increase in demand for insulation must have seemed like manna from heaven for the manufacturers and installers. Manufacturers geared up their production facilities to meet the huge demand. However, in a largely unregulated industry, unskilled and untrained workers were soon drafted into the insulation workforce, and four deaths resulted. The program was summarily cancelled in 2010, leaving manufacturers with millions of dollars tied up in excess stock and installers without jobs.

Therefore, as a prudent business owner, you need to be just as prepared for a downturn as you are for growth, because you just never know what may happen. The PESTLE analysis that you have already completed will hopefully point to some of the good and bad influences that can help or harm your business.

As a prudent business owner, you need to be just as prepared for a downturn as you are for growth.

SECTION 4
SIMPLIFY THE COMPLEXITY

"Organize around business functions, not people. Build systems within each business function. Let systems run the business and people run the systems. People come and go but the systems remain constant."
—Michael Gerber, The E-Myth Revisited

Every small business owner knows (or should know) that they need to have their business systemised. In fact, every business book worth its salt will tell you that you should be introducing, documenting, and developing systems within your business from day one. They talk about management systems, occupational health and safety systems, quality systems, environmental systems …

Back at the beginning of this book, I pointed out that if you want to reap the rewards of having a well-known brand on your customer list, you would have to make some changes. This section is about the most dramatic of those changes— **creating and documenting your business systems**.

Business systems can seem to be completely overwhelming, and many just find it too hard and walk away. I often use the analogy of a marathon runner with a sore knee. When the runner has a sore knee and they keep running, they certainly aren't giving themselves the best chance of winning. Getting your processes firmly in place and working for you is the business equivalent of fixing a sore knee.

Chapter 22
Why Your Business Needs Systems

There is a long and proud tradition of business books explaining the payoff from a properly systemised organisation. If you haven't read *The E-Myth Revisited* by Michael Gerber, one of the best-selling business books of all time, I recommend that you do so. In it, Gerber explains the value of sorting out your business structure, how to identify your personality type as a business person (personality types which Gerber characterises as Entrepreneur, Technician or Manager), how important it is to write up the processes of what you do, and why systems are so necessary.

However, even with the many great business books around, there is still an underwhelming range of sources describing exactly HOW to do this.

Starting the process of getting your business systems under control can seem overwhelming. Documenting everything you do? Where do you start? It all seems just so complex. And as noted in Chapter 12 most of us are one or two of these Entrepreneur, Technician or Manager types, and some—particularly those fitting the Manager type—will find it easier than others to undertake this necessary part of the business' growth and development. If you need assistance in this area, please don't underestimate the value in getting that help.

The truth is that you already HAVE systems in your business, but they may be quite rudimentary. Presumably things get done the same way (well, sort of) most of the time—or you wouldn't have any customers at all. Somehow, the message gets through to your team how things get done—mostly by word-of-mouth.

So, you have a system of sorts, but it's undocumented. As Michael Gerber notes, "If it's not in writing, it's not a system." So at this stage, you don't have a system, you have are undocumented processes.

Gerber also tells us that if you are in situation, you are likely tied so tightly to working IN your business that taking a break from it and having it function without you is virtually impossible. This in turn leads to a crisis of faith in your business' risk management—the one thing that is the most critical issue for big companies in the supply chain. If everything depends on you (and/or various critical people), the business is in grave danger if illness, or worse, strikes.

The Problem with Undocumented Processes

The problem with undocumented processes is that your tasks, simple or complex, just keep getting out of control. Every person will put their own twist on the way they perform a task, or they turn to cutting corners and shortcuts—leading to backlogs, work errors, missed deadlines, and more headaches. Education and psychology research tell us every person has the potential to understand a verbal instruction in a different way, and you will certainly have experienced this yourself. This introduces even more potential variability into the way a task is performed.

Every time you have a new employee start work or conditions change, the undocumented process usually changes as well. You find yourself repeating instructions over, and over, and over, and wondering why employees just can't do it right. I see this so often—the increasingly frustrated business owner who is at the point of just giving up. That one simple question keeps bothering them—how hard can it be to get a single employee or a team of employees to do the tasks correctly, the same way, every time?

What Exactly Do We Mean By "Systems"?

At this point, I would like to make clear what I mean by "systems". International consultancy firm McKinsey & Co. has what I believe is an excellent definition of business systems:

> "All the steps involved in creating and delivering a company's product."

For the purposes of this book, and in simpler language, a system is a way of doing things. The system allows us to get stuff done.

A system is a way of doing things. The system allows us to get stuff done.

Think about McDonald's. The success of that most famous of turn-key operations is as simple as ensuring that every single thing, including the number of steps it should take for an item to go from the freezer to the deep fryer, is written down. Absolutely nothing, regardless of how small, is left open to interpretation as to how it must be done.

Every uniform, order-taking procedure, order delivery, and even process of cleaning the restrooms is done in exactly the same way, all over the world.

Consistency is good for branding and image in any organisation. But it also means that there is no need for guesswork. Task management is so straightforward that anyone could do the task.

That's not to say that your company needs to be so carefully controlled at every level. Innovation and good ideas do need to be supported, but if you haven't got great systems that allow you to take time off from working in your business, then you don't really have a business, you just bought yourself a job!

Your business systems will consist of documented processes, procedures, and tasks, that are shared across the entire organisation, used and understood by everyone, and constantly reviewed and updated.

What Systems Are

Business systems are made up of living documents. By that I mean that they are continually updated as the business and the way things are done change.

They are used by everybody. They must capture what everybody does and uses, every day—how we do things around here. An independent test of how good your systems are is whether somebody who has never performed that task before could do it to an acceptable standard by following the documentation. This, of course, is what franchisors do so well. If I start work at a food franchise, I should be able to turn out food for customers that satisfy their requirements by following the documented system.

Systems are a set of building blocks that you will create and put together, and that all together describe exactly how your business operates. Ironically, in most businesses, it's when you get the systemisation up to a high level that innovation and great ideas flow and are easier to implement. Having systems and rules in place means that your team does not have to reinvent the wheel every time a procedure happens. Their time and mental capacity are freed to shift to a higher plane of creativity.

What Systems Are Not

Business systems are not a big folder of documents that have been printed out and then sit on a shelf that nobody touches. I see this so often when working with small businesses (and many large ones as well). I ask a business owner if they have documented systems, to which they reply "yes" and point to a dusty row of ring binders on the shelf in the corner of the office.

Business systems are not a sleep aid. I have seen many documented systems that seem to have been purposely designed to send any sane person to sleep, using complex and indecipherable language. The language must be appropriate, understandable, and user friendly.

Systems cannot be imposed from the top. When business systems are imposed from on high, without reference to and input from the people actually doing the tasks, they will almost always be ignored. Just as a river will find its own way around an obstacle, so will people find a way around inappropriate systems. Systems must therefore be shared across the entire organisation, used and understood by everyone. Everyone must have buy-in.

Systems, Processes, Tasks, and Procedures

If you stop to think about it, your entire business is a system. It is an interconnected set of activities and resources that has a defined outcome. What you are getting done is supplying a product or service that will solve a problem for your client. Hopefully it will make you a profit at the same time. Your business system is all the things you do to make that happen.

Let's take this back a step or two. The primary system that is your whole business is then made up of a lot of subsystems, and each of these subsystems has a purpose.

An excellent analogy is your car. You own a car to achieve a desired outcome—to transport yourself from one place to another in an efficient, timely, and convenient manner. The overall system of the car is made up of multiple other systems. There is a braking system, a steering system, a propulsion system, etc. All these individual systems work together to create the physical object and the experience of a car.

It is the same with your business. You have a finance system—where you or your bookkeeper enters invoices, payments, receipts, and payroll.

You have a human resources system, where you keep details about your employees and their performance.

You have a marketing system, where you attract potential buyers of your product/service, and convert them into paying customers.

And so on.

Each **system** is made up of a number of **processes**. Using the finance system as an example, there is a process to pay bills, a process to receive payments, a process to create invoices …

For each process, there will be a number of **tasks**. For every one of these tasks, there will be a **procedure** that documents how that task should be done.

The best way to illustrate how all this works is a diagram, using the finance system as an example:

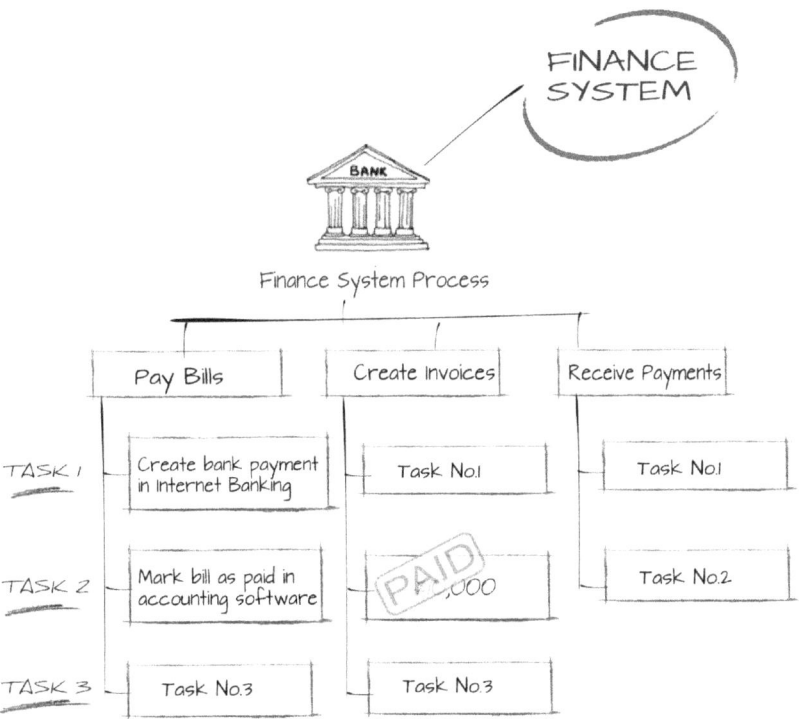

"System" Does Not Equal "Technology"

I want to clearly differentiate the business system from the technology used. For example, you might use the software Xero or MYOB to make your finance system easier to use. But you could also use paper and a pencil, or a series of Excel spreadsheets.

Same system, different technology.

Xero (or MYOB, or Excel, or your pencil and paper) isn't the finance system. It is simply the enabling technology.

Why Have Systems?

For many small business owners, the mere mention of business systems sends them into a cold sweat or a tirade of not very nice words. I once walked into a small business premises, and saw the following sign on what was obviously the storage cupboard for safety equipment. That particular proprietors' attitude to safety systems at least was summed up quite succinctly.

However, instead of thinking about documented business systems as a time-consuming, expensive, paper-wasting cost of doing business, you need to change your thinking around, and consider what having these systems in place could add to your business.

Chapter 23
The Business Benefits of Good Systems – the 5 Cs

Compliance

This book is about getting your small business ready to attract and work with big companies, and having good, documented systems is a ground-level requirement for dealing with all larger organisations. You simply will not be able to take on contracts with most large organisations without having certain systems implemented.

Compliance means having the minimum requirements in place and keeping them up to date. For example, it's no use proposing to build a bridge if you do not have properly qualified engineers on your team. That may seem to be a frivolous example, but compliance requirements can be reasonably simple (like having a qualified engineer) or amazingly complex (like a 20-step induction for visiting tradespeople). Unless you have all the minimum requirements in place, you are simply not going to get past the starting line. Having documented business systems will almost always form a part of these pre-qualification requirements, and those same systems will keep your compliance status current.

An excellent example is the pre-qualification required to work on a coal mining site. Apart from the professional qualifications required, everyone has to do a generic industry induction, then a site induction, and sometimes demonstrate that they have a site-driving licence. Then there is specific training depending on the work, such as working in confined spaces, working at heights, etc., and every vehicle and piece of equipment must be inspected and signed off. Vehicles have to have regular brake tests. It's not hard to see how complex this can become, particularly for a company that works on multiple sites. So, there has to be a system to get all this in place, and then to keep all the licences, inductions, and authorisations up to date.

Consistency

"It won't be done right."

How many times have you said to yourself or someone else, "I can't go away—it all goes pear shaped when I'm away and I spend days getting everything back on track."

Sometimes, as business owners, we have to get over our own ego, and implementing business systems is one of those occasions. You're the boss, so no-one else can do things as well you can, right? Wrong. Cemeteries are full of people who thought they were indispensable.

Once a system has been documented correctly, and the right people are trained or shown "how it works", there is no reason why things should be done incorrectly. That's right—you are not indispensable.

If you have to do everything yourself, your business will always be limited by the time that you have available, and you will forever have that feeling of being on the hamster wheel where you are constantly running and feeling exhausted, but not achieving a great deal. Remember Gerber's quote about your boss being an idiot if you can't step away from your own business for any period of time?

One of the reasons large organisations give for not using small suppliers is that they can't supply a consistent product or service all the time. Some days the quality is good, and some days it's not. Some days the delivery is on time, but on other days it's late. Systems ensure that the same thing is done in the same way, every time, on time. Again, think McDonald's.

Your customers don't want surprises. One of the mantras of large organisations as buyers is **DIFOT: delivered in full, on time**. Good systems allow you to do this, because everyone knows what should be happening, when, and how.

Cost

Let's continue with your finance system as an example. If you didn't have a finance system, it would be impossible to run your business, and the Tax Office would not be very forgiving. The finance system you have may be just the basics that you can get away with, such as what can fit onto an Excel spreadsheet. Or you could use the information that you legally have to keep (to pay your taxes and superannuation obligations) to give you a lot more knowledge about your business. For example, the kind of reports you can run using something like Xero or MYOB provide deep insights. Your systems will be providing you with all the vital information you need to make the best possible business decisions.

You can use this data to keep a close eye on your cash flow, profitability, stock levels, how long customers are taking to pay—and a whole lot more. In short, you can use the finance system to improve your business. And the same applies to all the other systems you need to have. In other words, using your systems to their full capacity will aid your profitability by giving you much greater insight into how your business is operating.

Cost is also closely related to consistency. Systems make your business so much more efficient, since they eliminate waste, rework, and rejects, and you don't have to reinvent the wheel or train someone every time a job needs to be done. Author Jay Arthur, in his book *Six Sigma Simplified: Quantum Improvement Made Easy*, has a wonderful way of describing this:

"Every company has two 'factories':
- *the 'Good' factory that creates and delivers your product or service*
- *and a hidden 'Fix-it' factory that cleans up all the mistakes and delays that occur in the main factory."*

FIX-IT-FACTORY

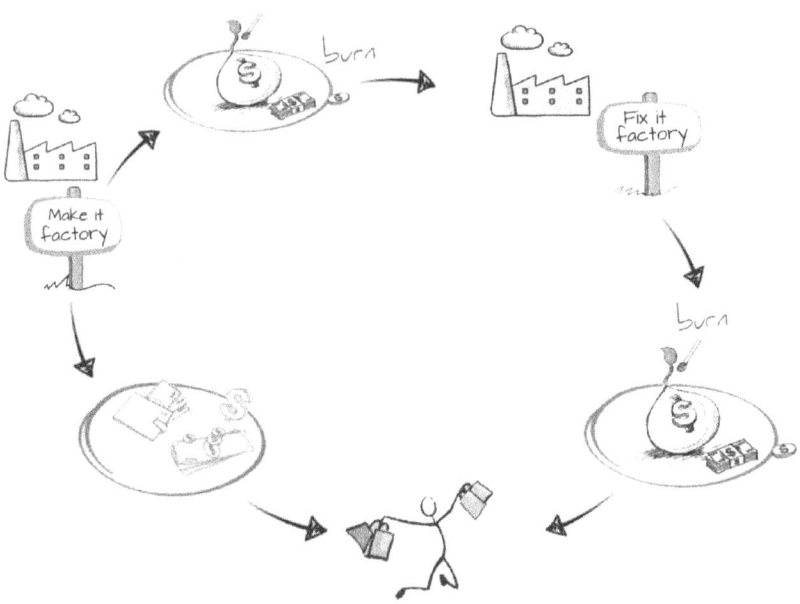

If you are running both these "factories", you are wasting time, money, and probably emotional energy repairing bad outcomes. Being efficient lowers your cost base, and makes you more competitive.

Control

"It's quicker to do it myself."

Have you ever caught yourself saying something like, "Why can't they do this right? I might as well just do this myself because no-one else can do this as well as I can." Or, "I can't get out of the office till 10 o'clock at night—I've just got to do everything."

This is the lament of the small business owner who feels that their business is constantly out of control, and I'd be willing to wager that you have said this yourself on more than one occasion: "It's just quicker to do it myself than to explain it all the time." Imagine how much time you could free up for yourself if you could:
- write down exactly what a task is and how it should be done
- train everyone how to do the task
- leave the documented procedure available for everyone to refresh their memory

By documenting your business systems, you're going to get yourself back in the driver's seat. Your team will know:
- what to do
- how to do it
- when to do it
- why it needs to be done

Even better, if someone else starts performing that task, they will probably find a better way of doing it than you.

Good, documented systems are also an asset to your business, just like the equipment you use and the people you employ. And just like your equipment and people, systems need to be put to work, not simply created and then left on the shelf. That would be like paying to hire a new accountant, and then putting them in the corner office with no work to do.

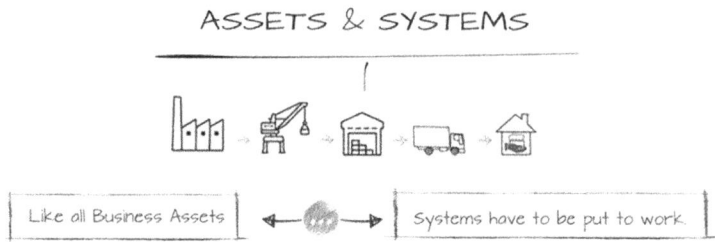

This is the fate of many turn-key systems documents that I see. A business owner buys, say, a "workplace health and safety system", loads it onto the computer or prints all the documents, ticks the "I've got a safety system" compliance box, and then never touches it again.

The "system" they bought bears no relation to what people in the business actually do, or even what they should do in some cases. What the system should do is document what *really happens—the procedures, methods,* processes, etc., that take place. Of course, you need to be sure that what they are doing is correct—the process of documenting your systems should identify any gaps between ideal behaviour and actual behaviour.

Create Value

The last "C" is perhaps the most often overlooked benefit, and it has a lot to do with the business exit. Not many business owners think about the business exit in the first flush of excitement when they're starting up a new business. Documenting your business systems to capture all your intellectual property creates value for when you finally choose to exit the business. Prospective buyers will be able to clearly see that the profit potential of the business doesn't walk out the door with you, and that future profitability can be maintained. Think about a McDonald's franchise. There is a reason why buying a McDonald's franchise is around three times more expensive to buy than other comparable franchise brands. The systems are proven, documented, and implemented consistently.

Good systems, documented and used well, will also undoubtedly increase your business profitability, naturally making it more attractive to a potential purchaser.

Chapter 24
The Seven Steps to Creating Systems

I noted previously that while every business guru on the planet will tell you that you must document your business systems, very few tell you how to actually go about it.

Over my years in business and dealing with big organisations, I have wasted untold hours trying various ways to get this done. After more false starts than I care to admit, I finally came up with seven steps that, I believe, cover the actual implementation phases.

Step 1: Pre-planning

The first step is pre-planning. If you have read, understood, and implemented the material in the Set Your Foundations section of this book (Section 3), you are well on your way. You will already have your business vision, your mission, your why, your value statements, and your business plan—and everyone on your team will understand and share these important drivers of your business.

This step is vital because without being very clear on these, you've got nothing to guide you as to the outcome of your systems.

> *"If you don't know where you are going, any road will get you there."* —*The Cheshire Cat, Lewis Carroll, Alice in Wonderland*

In the real world ...
In our consultancy, one of our driving values is scientific accuracy. We pride ourselves on 100% accuracy in our data management and reporting to our clients, so that the data the client receives is a 100% accurate reflection of the environmental situation that we found.

That desired outcome drives everything that is contained in our business systems. It drives who we hire, the brands of equipment we buy, the type of quotes and invoices we prepare, the way we check data and reports. If we didn't care what level of accuracy the client received—and believe me, there are some companies for whom that is the case—we could just hire some backpackers and dispense with all our data checking and data management procedures. We could simply get the data back from the laboratory or from our field tests and email it off to our clients, without any checking or interpretation. From our own research, we know that some 16% of laboratory reports contain an error that would compromise the clients' data set for decision making, so checking procedures is an integral part of supplying scientifically accurate reports.

This pre-planning stage is also where you, as the business owner, start keeping notes on what you do on a daily basis. Note down the things that you do, and how often they have to happen. Daily? Weekly? Monthly? As needed?

A notebook is ideal for this part of the process, or voice memos on your smart phone. Use an on-screen timer to actually start measuring and documenting what you do as a business owner. The reason it is important to do this is because at some point later on, you're going to be asking your team to do exactly the same thing. If you haven't done this yourself, you are not in a position to ask other people to do it, and advise them how. Walk around with a notebook, write down what it is you do during the day, or use some sort of time management software. It's important that you do this, because this is your first step into systems thinking.

A word of warning, though: make sure you share what you are doing with your team so they don't think you are (a) weird, or (b) spying on them.

Step 2: Get into the Systems Mood

The next step is to get your team on board with "systems thinking", so this is a team activity. The aim of these team sessions is to get everybody thinking of the business as a machine—a system. Using an analogy is good—something that relates to your business if you can come up with one. If you can't think of one, use the car analogy I described earlier. Everybody understands what a car is and basically how it works. Your team will all know that each part has to be working at its best for you to get to your destination fast, safely, and cost effectively.

You will need to have an agenda prepared to guide these team sessions, or they can very quickly go off the rails, because at this stage you will start to get objections—what I call ***push-back***.

"I'm too busy."

The first objection you will hear is "I'm too busy, I'm too busy doing my job to do this." I see a lot of business owners themselves in this mode. "I'm too busy to write all this stuff down. I'm too busy trying to earn money to do all this." This is a vicious circle. First, you're too busy to answer questions from an employee about how to do something. So, the employee does the best they can, which probably isn't what you had in mind. Your undocumented process results in uncontrolled design changes—where somebody unilaterally decides to change the process or skip a step. Then, someone has to fix the uncontrolled design changes, so they are now even busier, which leads to less control and even worse outcomes ... and so it goes on.

It is vitally important at this time that your team starts thinking of the WHOLE system as a machine—not just their individual silos. I will explain later how process outcome objectives can actually be in conflict with each other, and you have to have in the back of your mind the optimal performance of the whole system.

I'M AN EXPERT

"I'm an expert."

The next push-back you will hear is "I'm an expert, I know what I'm doing. I don't need a documented procedure to tell me what to do."

The subtext here is that your team experts see your documenting what they do as belittling, and that if their expertise is committed to paper, anyone will be able to do what they do and their source of power through knowledge will be diminished.

"I've done this a thousand times."

"Oh, I've done this a thousand times; I know what to do. I don't need to write it down."

This is a variation on the "I am an expert" narrative, but experts of all sorts have checklists for a very good reason (more on checklists later). Personally, I would not like an airline pilot to leave their pre-flight checklist in the departure lounge, saying, "Oh, I've done this a thousand times; I know exactly what to do," or a surgeon to not check all the machines that go *beep* when I'm having an operation.

You all know that things can be forgotten, and things do get forgotten. Sometimes, life just goes wrong.

> **In the Real World ... The Value of Checklists**
> *Years ago, my mum was going on a flight in a private aircraft. As they were preparing for take-off, the pilot didn't use the pre-flight checklist. On this light plane, there was a hook on the front wheel to tow the aeroplane out of the hanger and because the pilot skipped the pre-flight checklist, he didn't remove the hook. As soon as the plane was airborne, the propeller hit the steel hook and the pilot had to make a pretty hairy landing. Fortunately he was able to land again safely, and both the pilot and my mum were okay. I will never forget the horrible, sick feeling I had as I watched the event unfold, though.*

"Don't reduce my organisational power."

You won't hear this objection out loud, but it will be the motivator for some of the verbal excuses you will hear. Sometimes, team members will see documenting systems as decreasing their organisational power base. This is the person who has been with you for 20 years and knows everything, so nobody else can do that particular job (or jobs) except them. When you ask that person to document what it is that they do, they can see this as decreasing and eroding their power base. Incidentally, you are also addressing a critical risk in your business.

"Don't restrict my freedom."

The next resistance point you will hit is "Systems restrict my freedom and my creativity. How can I be creative and do my thing if I'm restricted by a procedure?"

The reality is that your written procedures act as a team of experts at your back. They capture the best knowledge about how your business should operate. Your documented procedures have got your back, giving you direction so that you don't have to think about routine things. Your mind is actually being given time to concentrate on the creative stuff.

Having a written procedure actually liberates rather than restricts.

I know there will be at least one genre of music that appeals to you—be it rock, jazz, country, classical or something else. One of my favourite pieces of music is Johann Sebastian Bach's Concerto for Violin and Oboe, Third Movement. You may not be a fan of classical music, but there's a reason that this is still popular after several hundred years. It is a superbly crafted composition and, to me, sublime. I don't believe that anyone could reasonably argue that Bach was not creative. But the exquisite, creative expression in that music actually follows rules. There are rules of composition, and anyone who is musically trained will know those rules. But for those of us who don't know the rules, we just hear the beautiful, creative end result. Rules and procedures do not restrict our creativity. Bach did not have to devise the rules of composition every time he sat down at the piano. He used those procedures, discovered and documented by others, to create his own, unique musical offering.

Step 3: Take the Helicopter View

Imagine you are looking down on your business from above, and visualise all the parts—the systems that make up your business. What does each part do, what is its objective, and how do all the parts fit together? This is a group activity, and is extremely important. It must be given priority, without being interrupted by the daily busyness around you. Set a time, stick to it, and make sure everyone turns up.

The best way to start this activity is with a whiteboard and coloured sticky notes. Colour code each of the different systems you identify, so finance might be green, human resources blue, and administration yellow, etc. This may have to be done over several sessions so that the entire team is tuned in to what you are trying to achieve. Leave at least one hour for the first session, and you should make good progress.

Once you have identified all of your company's component systems, you can now start adding sticky notes for each of the processes within that system, and name them. Take your HR systems as an example. Perhaps you have a recruitment process, an induction process, and a disciplinary process. Add a sticky note of the appropriate colour for each of these processes.

"If you can't describe what you are doing as a process, you don't know what you're doing. 94% of all failure is a result of the system ... not people."
—*W. Edwards Deming*

Each process should have a single objective. The objective of your recruitment process, for example, will be to recruit team members with the required skills, attitudes, and values to fit with your company. Sometimes, however, the objectives of two processes can be in conflict.

> **In the real world ...**
> In our consultancy business, we aim to issue a certain type of report within five days. That is the objective of one process, and we measure and report on that. At the same time, there is a report checking process with a desired outcome of 100% accuracy. The two objectives are in conflict. We could easily meet the first objective by simply writing the report quickly and sending it on to the client. However, without the report checking step, the objective of 100% accuracy will not be achieved.

This small example shows why it is so important to have everyone involved, and thinking outside their silos. Only then will you be able to identify where the linkages and possible conflicts arise.

Step 4: Prioritise

This is where you get to take the lead role again, as the business owner. At this stage, you and your team are most probably staring at the whiteboard covered in coloured sticky notes, and feeling completely overwhelmed. Where on earth should you start to create some order out of the tangle of systems and processes you have just created?

My suggestion is that you start with the things that drive you nuts—your real pain points. There will always be a couple of things in your business that really get on your nerves, and/or cost a lot of money. In our consultancy business, my number one trigger point was people going out to do field work but forgetting some of the equipment. It drove me insane, and it also cost a lot of money because somebody else would have to stop what they were doing and drive out to deliver the missing items.

While you need to address your most painful blisters first, you also want to score a few "quick wins". Having a few successes right off the bat is a very powerful way of getting the team on board. Make a list of 10–20 issues in your business that come to mind, and put them into one of these four categories:

- Quick wins. You can solve these easily and quickly and keep the systemisation project momentum going.
- Critical to the business. Which issues are costing you the most time and dollars? If you get these things right, your business will benefit immediately.
- Bottlenecks, or just driving you nuts. Where are the bottlenecks in your workflow, or the things that happen over and over again—incorrectly?

- Big payoff, but not necessarily critical to the business. Like quick wins, these issues are not critical to the business, but will make a material difference when the change is made.

While you are doing this keep the Pareto principle (the 80/20 rule) in mind: 20% of the sticky notes that you put up in step three will be the ones causing you 80% of your problems.

Step 5: Flowcharting Your Systems

This step gets a bit technical, and you may have to ask for help. Even though you and your team will have to do some hard thinking, do not skip this step. This is where most systemisation projects (and indeed most "business improvement" projects) fail—at the point where some real effort is required.

For each of the systems and subsystems you have identified, you will now need to break it down into its component tasks.

Flowcharting can be as easy or as difficult as you want to make it. The simplest way is to return to your whiteboard (make sure you capture your initial work from Step 3 by photographing it first before you dismantle it). You can use butcher's paper and markers, sticky notes on a wall, or one of the many free software programs available online. I'm not going to include a lesson in flowcharting in this book because there are thousands of resources online that you can turn to.

Flowcharts are a visual representation of a process. There is a start, a finish, things to do, and decision points, and that's all you have to capture: what initiates the process (the starting point), what gets done, what decisions have to be made, and how the process ends.

Don't be concerned if you think you are capturing either too much or not enough detail at this stage, as you will review and refine your flowcharts later. If you can capture 80% to 90% of the process at this stage, you are on track for success.

Example: Flowchart of the collections process.

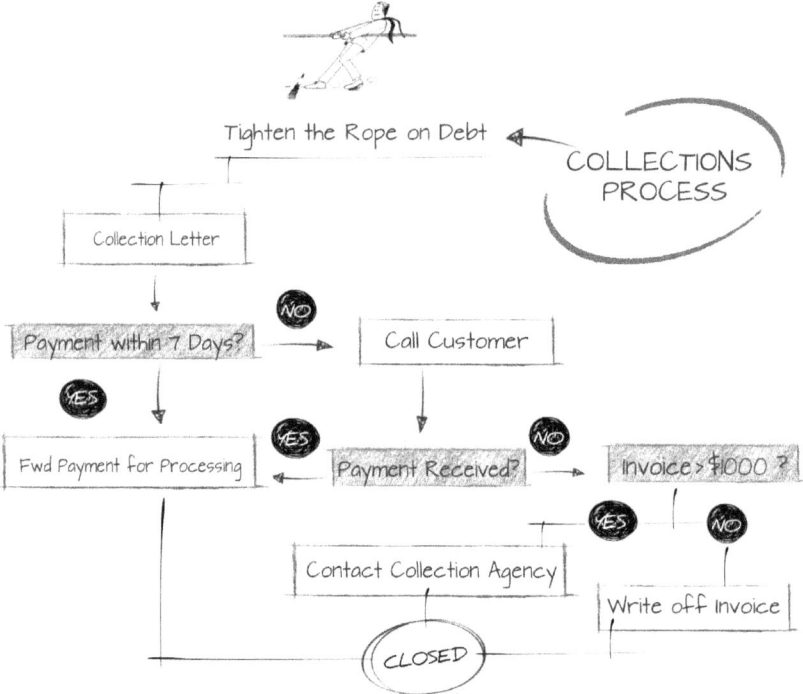

Step 6: Document the Tasks

Notice how we have made it to the sixth step of a seven-step process before we even start writing procedures? This is one of the main reasons why most business systemisation projects fail. Everybody wants to jump straight to the writing bit, because that's the easy part. When my children were in primary school, I would volunteer as a parent helper for an annual drama competition. The kids had to create a short play on a given theme. They had to come up with an idea, create a scenario, write the script, and then create their props, costumes, etc., from scrap materials. The kids always wanted to get straight into building the props and costumes—creating, painting, pasting, and generally having a fun time. The teachers and adult helpers always had to drag them back to the beginning of the process, and come up with an idea, an outline of their play, characters, etc., that would dictate the costumes and props they needed. Your team will probably be the same as the primary school children and want to dive right in to the writing part without completing the preparatory work.

Start creating your documents using simple document creation software like Microsoft Word to start with. The technology platform can be chosen later. Starting the capture process is the most important at this stage.

While writing down a procedure for completing a task may seem to be very simple, I see many more badly written procedures than I see good ones. Have you ever purchased an appliance or piece of equipment, opened the instruction manual, and immediately felt a headache coming on? The instructions are so complicated, long, and downright confusing, that you really feel like returning it for an immediate refund.

Unfortunately, I see far too many documented company procedures that must have been prepared from the same template as those instruction manuals—designed to actually stop people from performing their tasks, rather than making them easier. I call this the "procedures by the kilo" approach. Procedures are the "how to" for completing a simple task or a complex process. In short, documented procedures are the building blocks of your business. You put them all together, and they describe exactly how your business should be operating. But what makes a good procedure good?

Assign a project manager

This person will be in charge of the writing phase –making sure that somebody is assigned to writing all the procedures. This may be you, but you can delegate, and then bring it all together yourself at the end.

Make a template

Create a procedure for writing procedures. Humans are creatures of habit, so use consistent formatting, fonts, bolding, etc., so that the format is standard across everything. Even small decision tasks take time and energy, so having a standard format will help anyone using the procedure in the future. Include a purpose of the procedure, maybe some background information, who it applies to, and then the procedure. Check out the Small Company, Big Business website for example templates to follow.

Do some yourself

While you do have a project manager now, take the time to document some procedures yourself in the beginning. I always find it's easier to get people to provide feedback on something I've done than to get them to start something from the ground up themselves. You are more likely to get suggestions for improvement if you provide a framework and an example.

Capture what actually happens in your business—or at least what should happen

I recently met a business owner who downloaded a $6,000 "health and safety system", but it bore absolutely no relation to how health and safety was actually managed in her business (or not managed). Under current WHS law, having that "safety system" would not protect that business owner from prosecution. This is especially so in jurisdictions where Workplace Manslaughter laws have been brought in. A folder on the shelf will not protect you from jail. A good procedure must mirror the daily experiences of the business—what everyone does and uses. Include ALL the steps, even the small ones. No matter how small, it may be the critical missing link if it's not there.

Dot points are ok
Contrary to popular practice at the big end of town, procedures do not have to be long and complicated. For most small businesses, much will be captured with simple numbered lists or dot points.

Don't assume knowledge
Be aware of making assumptions in your procedures. It's easy to do. If you find yourself saying, "But everyone knows that," think again. Do they really? I once attended a workshop on preparing tenders for a particular large company. To illustrate the point that we should not assume knowledge when preparing tender documents, we were asked to write a procedure to sort a deck of cards in suit and number order. Try it yourself. Remember, no assumptions. The person reading your procedure does not know what a deck of cards is, what a suit is, what Ace, King, Queen and Jack cards are … Give yourself 10 minutes and try this yourself. It will be good practice.

Start with checklists
Checklists are the best. Look around your business and see what procedures can be captured by a simple checklist as they are the easiest to prepare. If steps have to be done in a particular order, make sure you number them.

Do not re-write War and Peace
How long should a procedure be? The answer is—exactly how long it takes to clearly guide the reader through the task. No shorter, and no longer. Anyone who has dealt with large corporations will have encountered this, where every procedure reads like someone swallowed and then regurgitated a management textbook. Just get to the point. Procedures are not the place to practice your creative writing skills, either.

Give your procedures short, descriptive titles

At some point, someone in your team will go searching for a procedure, so the title needs to be appropriate. Think of it like a Google search—what would people look for?

Action-oriented wording

A good procedure shows both the outcome and what actions to take, step by step. Use action words like "must", "shall", and "will". If you feel the urge to write "should", stop. What you are about to write probably shouldn't be in there at all, but be included with the supporting material.

Identify all the associated documents and resources

By associated documents I mean any forms, scripts, worksheets, dashboards, job descriptions, etc., that relate to the procedure. I recall one of my business mentors telling me that he has a 45,000 word script for use in his sales conversations. This would be included as an associated document, as would any worksheets for calculations, dashboards, equipment manuals, etc.

Avoid duplication

Duplicated procedures is something that I see a great deal of, where several people have created a procedure for the same thing, all filed in a different place. Return to your helicopter view step, and identify the places where your processes touch each other and the linkages they have. I used an example earlier of paying your bills on internet banking. Presumably, the wages and the Tax Office are also paid by internet banking, so it makes sense to have just one procedure for creating internet banking payments, not three. Then, if something changes, or you start using a different bank, you only have to update one procedure and avoid having conflicting documents.

Set goals

Set some goals with your project manager to make sure the project continues. Even if you aim to achieve just one documented procedure per week, or even one per month, having a target will keep the momentum going.

Step 7: Refine and Review

Once you have completed your helicopter view mapping and flowcharts, and built up a significant amount of documentation, you may be tempted to think that you have finished, and all that is left to do is to print off all the documents, put them in a folder, and put it on a bookshelf.

Wrong. At this point you've actually only just started.

Each procedure must be peer reviewed by someone who is not familiar with the task. Get them to complete the task using the procedure. This will detect all the missing or incomplete elements—things such as:
- assumptions made
- steps missed out
- terminology not defined
- unclear instructions
- steps not in a logical sequence

> **In the real world ...**
> In our consultancy company, we have a dashboard that we use for our monthly reports. I had always been the one to update the dashboard, but eventually I decided that this task should be outsourced. I created a set of
>
> >>

> *procedures for my virtual assistant, Janice, that I thought were perfectly self-explanatory. The first time I asked Janice to do the monthly update, she came straight back with about 10 questions asking what I meant. I had been doing that task for probably a decade, so I knew exactly what I was talking about, but I hadn't proofed or field tested the procedures with anybody else. It wasn't until I sent it to Janice (who also has English as a second language) that I realised that my procedures simply weren't clear enough.*

Now that you have made a start, your documentation journey can continue unabated. Please don't let all your good work to date go to waste by letting the project flag. You must now build the use of these procedures into your everyday activities. Everybody must follow the procedures. In our office, whenever somebody asks a question, the first reply is always, "Have you checked the procedure?" The intent behind this question is to make people think about what they are doing, and if we come across something that isn't documented, it gets documented.

The flip side of enforcing procedures is that your team must be empowered to update procedures when necessary. This is the release valve for changes, to prevent those undocumented design changes that I mentioned earlier. This is the mistake that I see in large companies and government departments. Nobody is empowered to make changes and the system does not allow for suggestions to travel upwards in the organisation. All direction comes from the top. Then, when a procedure differs from everyday practice, people will find a way around the obstacle.

> **In the real world ...**
> I met Jan at a business breakfast. Jan worked for the public service in a client service role where she would visit families in financial distress. Her territory covered a huge area—some 60,000 square kilometres. One of her performance metrics was the number of face-to-face hours spent with clients, but this performance management procedure had been put in place by someone who clearly had no concept of remote areas. Jan was not permitted to count her travel time as part of her face-to-face hours. Being an innovative person, Jan came up with the idea of using Skype to meet with those clients who had internet access, and promptly started to install Skype on her work laptop that she was required to use for all client communications—presumably for privacy reasons. However, yet another procedure prevented her from installing any third party software on a work computer. There was only one solution for Jan—to install Skype on her personal iPad and connect with her clients from there. Technically, Jan was disobeying several procedures, but she was managing to achieve the desired outcome of more time spent helping her clients.

If significant changes are required, the entire team (or part of a team) should be consulted, perhaps at your next team meeting. Step back to the helicopter view and the flowchart, then allocate the re-writing task to someone who will submit the revised procedure to the team for review.

Schedule updates and reviews on a regular basis, just to make sure that everything is still as it should be. I like to set a target of reviewing every procedure every 180 days. We don't always make it, but that is our aim.

Lastly, make sure that you inform people of changes. This can be done in a number of ways, including by email notification or at regular team meetings.

Chapter 25
The Technology Question

In this world of supplying to large organisations, you will have to comply with the formal systems documents that your customer requires, especially when you start mapping to or being certified against the international standards (more on international standards later, page 178).

Part of these requirements will be to record *who has created and who has approved the documents (**authorisation control**)*. However, even if you're not going down the road of being certified to international standards, I highly recommend that this be included in your system documentation.

Associated with authorisation control is ***version control***— being able to track versions as the procedure or process is updated. Again, I believe that this is an important quality control for yourself. Knowing and tracking when procedures have been updated, and keeping some brief notes on why changes were made, will ensure the internal quality control of your system documentation.

Of course, you can do all this in Word documents and other manual documentation systems using document properties, headers and footers, etc., and many large companies are still using Word for their entire systems documentation. But there are so many other options available now at a very reasonable cost that automatically take care of the version control and authorisation control, and more appear on the market regularly. Many of these platforms allow for hyperlinking between documents to easily solve the problem of duplicate documents (simply hyperlink from one document to another) and quick links to external documents. If you are serious about your document systemisation project, make the commitment to using a purpose-built platform rather than trying to track multiple Word documents.

Every person should have easy access to the procedures they need for their tasks. If not, don't be surprised when they aren't complying with procedures. I have seen far too many documented systems where there is an agglomeration of Word documents on a server somewhere and "I know we wrote something about that somewhere but I can't remember where we have filed it" is a common refrain. Every person trying to access a procedure has to question whether this is the latest version written by the subject expert, or just a few notes that someone made and filed in the same folder.

Using a purpose-built software solution avoids all that delay, confusion, and potential errors. After all, that is what we are trying to achieve by implementing systems in the first place.

"Why do you do it this way? If your employees can't answer how something they do helps the customer or the company, you've insulated your people from their jobs."
—Seth Godin[24]

---

24 Seth Godin, "Why Do You Do It This Way?", Seth's Blog, last updated May 18, 2015, http://sethgodin.typepad.com/seths_blog/2015/05/why-do-you-do-it-this-way.html.

The Perfect Checklist?

I'm a great fan of checklists. Such a simple tool can make such a difference to your business. Back when I was describing the seven steps of a systemisation project (Chapter 24), I mentioned that one of the things that really bugged me was people heading out into the field but leaving equipment they needed behind. The solution was checklists for each project: a simple laminated A4 piece of paper with a list of the required items so each item required could be ticked off as it was loaded.

There is no fool-proof way to design effective checklists, or method to keep them updated. Businesses differ, and so do the tools and devices they employ. However, there are some sound principles that you should adhere to when preparing checklists for your business.

- It has a clear purpose, and the purpose is stated. What is this checklist for? What problem is it preventing?
- It is short. Once you've gone over one page, ask yourself if it should be split into two or more lists, or if it has redundant items.
- It uses simple language and fonts. There's no place for flowery sentences or fancy fonts here.
- It covers a task that is important. It might be a repetitive task that has been done a thousand times, but if it's not done properly or completely, there are financial or other consequences.
- It requires the user to physically check a box or write something. The physical act of writing or checking a box helps you to stay on-task. (Believe me, there's a whole body of research around this.)
- It is formatted logically. The user doesn't have to jump from the top to the bottom and back again while completing the list.
- If tasks have to be performed in a certain order, number them sequentially in the correct order. If there is no particular order, simply use dot points.

- It has been "stress-tested" or peer-reviewed by actual users, and altered to reflect their input.

While it's great to have technology options, remember that in some instances, for some things, a paper-based model is still a good, straightforward option. Batteries run out of juice far more often than pens run out of ink, and paper can be much easier to use in high heat or humidity than tablets.

Chapter 26
Do I Need to be Certified?

Do I Need to Have a Quality Certification?

It depends. If you are supplying (or trying to supply) to a big company or a government department, you may find that they require you to have ISO 9001 Certification before they will do business with you at all. (This should be one of the first things to check in potential contracts.) For any small business that is not certified, this requirement is, of course, a disqualifier—unless they are prepared to go on the certification journey.

To become certified, you will probably have to engage a consultant to make sure you are ready for your audit, and then pay for the audit itself. There will then be ongoing costs to keep your certification up to date, so the process can be a significant cost item for a small business. However, if not being certified is holding your business back and stopping you from getting contracts, then yes, it is worth the cost. Having ISO 9001 certification will also help you when you are completing tender documents. There will usually be a question something like this one:

"Is your firm accredited to ISO 9001 by an approved certification body?"

If you answer no to this question, you will have to then answer a series of questions about your approach to managing quality. If you answer yes, you skip to the next section, saving yourself a significant amount of time.

And I don't mean "certified insane", although I sometimes do wonder about the sanity of anyone who starts and operates a small business. There are **various ISO (International Organization for Standardization) standards for quality, environmental, safety, and risk management systems.** The ISO is an independent body that establishes world-wide standards for all sorts of things to ensure consistency across all countries. Apart from having to have certain academic or industry qualifications, the most common pre-qualification request will be to have a documented quality, safety, risk management, and environmental system. All these standards are based on the methodology illustrated below.

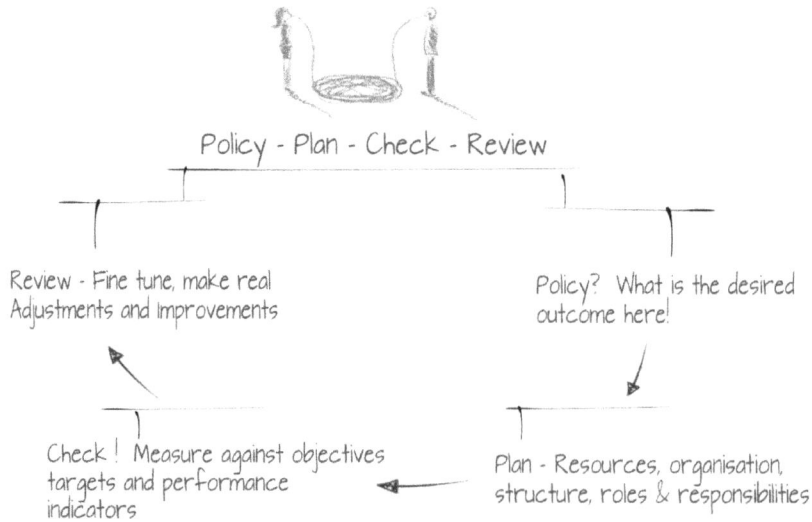

The first one you will be asked for is your quality system. In my experience though, many small business owners don't really know what a quality standard is, or worse, think that it's just another load of paperwork that they have to do.

What is a Quality Standard?

Every business owner knows that meeting customer expectations is a key pillar of business success. A ***quality standard*** is a template for doing just that—helping you meet your customers' expectations.

Quality doesn't necessarily mean the best possible, or most expensive. "Quality" in this context means that it meets the customers' expectations and requirements—consistently. By this definition, McDonald's runs a high-quality operation. I'm sure it wouldn't be hard for you to name a burger joint that serves more delicious (and expensive) burgers than anything you can buy at McDonald's. At McDonald's, however, you know exactly what to expect and how much you will pay, and you will get the same product every time. That is what the ISO standard means by "Quality".

> *"Quality in a product or service is not what the supplier puts in. It is what the customer gets out and is willing to pay for." —Peter F. Drucker*

Does a Quality Standard Tell Me How to Make Quality Products?

The answer to this question is a definite NO. The quality standard ISO 9001:2015 is just the framework, and it's up to you to fill in the details about ***how you manage and control quality*** in your own operations.

> *The quality standard merely tells you how to build your own quality management system, not how to actually make quality products.*

Using the framework provided by the standard, you will write your own procedures, policies, and processes that explain:
- your company's approach to quality
- how you design and build quality into all your products and services
- how you measure quality
- what action you will take when things don't quite go to plan

Having a quality management system doesn't mean that you have some procedures that you downloaded from the internet in a folder somewhere. It also doesn't have to be complex and run to hundreds of pages. Keep it simple and practical, so it describes what happens in *your* business.

Once you have this in place, you can then choose to be audited by a qualified professional, and achieve ISO9 001 certification. But you don't have to.

Certified vs. Compliant

Having that auditor's tick will make you ISO 9001 certified. Alternatively, you could choose to not have the audit, but still be ISO 9001 compliant. To be compliant, you would use the ISO framework to build your quality management system, and implement it well.

Being ISO 9001 compliant is definitely a good idea. Being able to write in proposals that your company is "ISO 9001 compliant" will give you an advantage over your competitors when you prepare proposals and tenders.

If you have thought about your approach to quality and how you will maintain your quality standards, there is a 100% chance that your business will be running a whole lot smoother, your costs from waste and returns will plummet, and your customers will be satisfied. They will be getting exactly what they ordered, with no surprises.

Safety

The next system your potential big customer will be looking for is your safety system—how you manage the safety of your employees and everyone who does business with you. To the companies you are targeting, safety can be a massive expense. Even near misses can cost hundreds of thousands or more in lost productivity. William Pegg, author of the book *Changing the Game: Rewriting the Rules for Mid-Market Procurement*, put it this way: "If there is the slightest whiff of you not taking safety seriously, you WON'T get in the door." Unfortunately, for too many small business owners, safety is nothing but a costly nuisance, and I often wonder how we got to this point of viewing the responsibility for human safety and well-being as nothing but an impost. The reason to be safe at work has more to do with you and your family's future, and less to do with the completion of your daily tasks.

The truth is that managing safety in your business doesn't have to be a complicated affair. You do have to comply with the appropriate legislation, but at its heart, safety management comes down to just these questions:

- What could happen that could hurt me or someone else?
- What would the consequence be?
- What can I do prevent that happening?

Yes, you will have to document something that is more formal than those three questions, and again, I urge you to write down exactly what happens in your business. If you haven't had these conversations with your team, have them now. Every state government in Australia provides free training and resources that will help you along your way. You can also have a safety inspector come to your business to help you identify problems and solutions. There are also resources on the Small Company, Big Business website that I have found helpful over the years and I'm happy to share.

Chances are though that your big customer won't have a simple safety system. I heard a speaker at a forum share her experience of dealing with her large customer. She had 14 separate contracts with one company, which is a wonderful achievement on her part. However, the customer's safety system had required them to complete the pre-qualification documents all 14 times. For every one of those 14 contracts, the same set of pre-qualification documents had to be submitted. Seemingly, they had no way of relating one contract to any other, creating an enormous amount of work for the supplier.

In the words of another small business owner, "Half the time the big companies themselves don't know what they want." This can be extraordinarily frustrating to you as a business owner, and goes at least some of the way towards explaining why there is a great deal of negative feeling towards implementing safety systems and safe work procedures.

Interestingly, when I conducted some research of my own on small business attitudes to workplace safety, cost didn't figure as a problem. In short, engaged business owners do not have a problem with the cost of being safe. What they do have a problem with, however, is costs that are imposed, but don't actually contribute to safety. Some of the comments I received show that not all small business owners have a negative attitude to the safety of their team and others who do business with them.

"Safety is incorporated in the company's financial budget."

"Safety brings confidence and motivation in workers."

"Lack of safety at a work place can actually turn out to be so costly to an organisation."

Risk

Back in Section 2, I emphasised the importance of continually assessing your external environment for events or trends that could impact upon your business. I also introduced the concept of portfolio risk—having all your eggs in one basket. Both these subjects are concerned with business risk. Your health and safety system will also consider risk, but the risk of harm to people. Your environmental management system (page 184) addresses any risk to the environment from your activities.

So, risk is present right through your organisation. Like your safety system, your risk management system will identify what could go wrong, what would happen if it does go wrong, and how you are going to prevent it. In fact, I have written an entire book on this topic of managing risks in a small business—*Small Company, Big Crisis: How to Prepare for, Respond to, and Recover from a Business Crisis*. You can get details about this book on page 281.

If this is the first time you have actually thought through what risks face your business, I've provided a few questions that will get you thinking.

 RISK

- The Government changed a law that severaly impacted your business?
- Currency exchange rates changed dramatically ... increasing costs?
- There was a natural disaster like a flood, cyclone, or fire?
- Your key employee resigned?
- You were taken ill and could no longer work?
- You had a massive computer failure and lost key records.

Of course you won't be able to foresee every risk that your business faces. Things just happen sometimes. It's called Murphy's Law. However, you can certainly minimise the impact of Murphy's Law by thinking ahead, identifying as many risks as you can, and putting plans in place to deal with them—your Recovery Plans.

I highly recommend you read my book *Small Company, Big Crisis* to fully understand your risk, and management options for risk in your business. At the very least, log onto the questionnaire you can find on my website, go to a quiet corner somewhere as soon as possible, and think through each of these questions. Your ability to answer them is one thing, but being ready for any of these situations takes serious thinking, and **having a risk management plan in place is critical to your long term success—not to mention your peace of mind and the security of those who depend upon you**.

Environmental

The last of the "big four" management systems is your ***environmental management system (EMS)***. Everything you do as a business will have some impact on the environment. Even driving to work every day will contribute to carbon emissions. Your environmental management system details how you are going to measure and manage your environmental impacts. Specifically, it will show how you are going to:

- comply with any legislation that is applicable
- minimise your environmental impact and prevent any incidents that would harm the environment
- improve your environmental performance over time

Like all the other management systems, implementing a good EMS will also help your company. You will both reduce costs and maximise profit. Again, to get you started, I have included a few questions for you to answer.

- Do you use any hazardous materials or chemicals in your operations?
- Do you generate waste, off-cuts, or reject products?
- What happens to your products after your customers have finished with them?
- How much energy do you use (including electricity, gas, petrol, diesel)?
- How much paper do you use per month/year?

As at the middle of 2023, as I'm preparing the second edition of this book, many countries and companies around the world are committing to low or zero emissions. This is having a huge impact on various industries.

SECTION 5
MAKE YOURSELF KNOWN

When interviewing small business owners for this book, one of the main challenges that people mentioned to me was how hard it is to get noticed. My research showed that 65% of small business owners found that getting noticed by their potential big clients is a significant hurdle for them.

This was not exactly news to me, as I have struggled with that same problem in our own businesses. How do you actually get that first contract with a big buyer? This section is not intended to be a sales training program. There is an enormous amount of material written and available in publications and various training programs on the sales process, and how to improve your sales skills, and I have listed some of my favourite resources on the Small Company, Big Business website. In this section, I will cover the very first steps you must take if you want to get on the radar of your potential large customers.

Chapter 27
To Be or Not to Be—Online

If you're not online, you don't exist.

Many small business owners are still coming to grips with the myriad of ways to engage with digital marketing. The old forms of marketing that have served you well—perhaps for decades—just don't work on their own anymore, and you may have had to go on a fast and steep learning curve about websites, Facebook, Twitter, LinkedIn, and all the rest. Having said that, there are companies going back to using paper-based or physical marketing tools because the digital landscape has become so crowded and noisy.

The quote at the beginning of this chapter, though, is absolutely true. If you're not online, you're nowhere, because that is the first place your potential big client is going to look to either find you or check you out. Think back to the last time you heard about someone of interest or met a new contact at a networking event? Did you check them out on LinkedIn or did you Google them?

In short, you need to have a credible digital footprint which is made up of the trails and tracks you leave on the internet. This is what others can find out about you online. It will feature your website, social media profiles (Facebook, LinkedIn, Twitter, Instagram, etc.), comments in forums and on others' posts, and virtually anything else you do online. Also if you have been mentioned in any news items at any time this is also likely to come up in a Google search. Remember that this includes both your company and personal profiles. In this day and age, any and all prospective customers will be forensically examining your digital footprint for clues as to whether to do business with you.

At the time of writing this book, we know that when buyers are looking for professional service providers, eight out of ten of them look at the website of their potential suppliers.[25] Having said that, the social media space has become so crowded and noisy, that some innovative marketers are returning to snail-mail (letters), printed catalogues and traditional marketing. It's a constantly evolving scene!

Less than 1% of buyers say that they don't check out their potential suppliers.

Don't leave this to chance. Take control over your marketing. If you have a website and some social media profiles that are well managed and look professional, you are able to manage the perception of how others see you online when they go looking. Large companies repeatedly report that often, even if they do want to find and engage small suppliers, they lack professionalism in their marketing, and are therefore all but invisible.

The two main deficiencies cited by large purchasers are:
- no professional email address
- no website

So these are the big issues that I want to address in this section.

---

25   Hinge Research Institute, *Beyond Referrals: How Today's Buyers Check You Out*, 2014, https://hingemarketing.com/library/article/beyond-referrals-how-todays-buyers-check-you-out.

Chapter 28
Your Email Is a Big Part of Your Brand

What these big companies mean by no professional email address is finding a business using free email providers such as Gmail, Yahoo, Hotmail, BigPond etc., so that their email address appears as, say, john@yahoo.com, or ABCservices@hotmail.com.

Your Free Email Could be Costing You More Than You Realise

The most common reason for small businesses to be using a free email address is just that—it's free. Every small business owner knows that saving costs where you can is an important element of success. But in the big scheme of things, the amount of money required to set up your own email domain (that's the bit after the @ symbol) is miniscule when compared to the benefits. Your email address is an integral part of your company's brand—what people think of when they think of your company.

Think about Coca-Cola. The logo includes the word Coca-Cola

written in white on a coloured (red for classic Coke) background. The *word* Coca-Cola lets you know what you are about to drink, but it conveys so much more. In fact, the company was responsible for the red Santa suit that started to be used in Christmas-related marketing images in the late 1800s. Coca-Cola's exact shade of red is not only trademarked, but its subtly tied into the joy of Christmas. This is about reinforcing their brand values of happiness, spontaneous fun, refreshment, optimism, friends sharing joy, etc. … The Coca-Cola Company is highly protective of its brand and its brand images. Their classic bottle is also patented, and it is no accident that Coca-Cola is consistently named as the world's most valuable brand.

Coca-Cola, like most companies, has recognised that their brand is much more than a symbol or logo. The company has clearly expressed its values, and everything the company does reinforces those values—the ads, the events it sponsors, even the causes it chooses to support.

The same applies to your small business. Every external expression of your brand is conveying something about your company. It's in the selection of what colours are shown on your signage, how the drivers of your company vehicles behave and the way your people wear their branded uniforms.

Eight Key Reasons Your Email Is an Integral Part of Your Brand

You want to look modern

You may have had your free business email address since the dawn of the internet age. By keeping it, however, you simply look outdated to your prospective customers. You would look very old-fashioned sporting that brick-sized mobile phone that you had in the 1980s. You need to update your email as well.

You want to look professional
Having a free email address gives the impression that you are not prepared to spend money on something as important as your brand. The buyer will wonder whether that same attitude applies to your goods and services. Will your products and services be reliable and of sufficient high quality for their purposes?

It enhances your credibility
Large buyers devote so much effort to scrutinising their suppliers to avoid risk. As you have already seen, they hate risk in their supply chains, and the risk of a supplier disappearing is a critical consideration for them. You are asking them to trust you as a reliable and credible supplier, but having a free email address makes you look as though you're not an established, credible business.

You can build marketing opportunities within your footnotes
With every email you send, you can remind the reader about your business. As a business owner, you need to take every opportunity you possibly can to make people aware of your business name and brand. BigPond, Hotmail and Gmail don't need your help to promote their brands.

You want to be taken seriously
Registering your own domain name (again, that's the bit after the @ symbol) for your website means you automatically can have your emails as Jake@ or Info@ or Admin@ <mybusinessname.com>. This is neither expensive nor hard to do. By not bothering to take this basic step, you are telegraphing that you are not serious about your business. If you won't take your own business seriously, you certainly cannot expect your big company prospects to do so.

Your emails avoid most spam filters

Free email services are used by spammers to send thousands of fake or malicious emails. So much so that many large organisations simply block traffic from addresses like @Hotmail, @Yahoo, or @Gmail. Your email many not even arrive in your prospect's inbox, and instead will be trapped by a junk filter, never to be seen again.

Strength against hackers

I'm no tech geek, but my friends who are assure me that by having a free email address, you are more vulnerable to hackers. Your big company client will not be happy if your unsecured systems mean that you are exposing them to potential attack as well.

You significantly increase your chances of success

Research has shown that your big company prospect is nine times more likely to choose a company with its own email domain over one with a free email address.

Chapter 29
Your Website

Just like your email address, your website is also a part of your brand. It doesn't have to be all-singing, all-dancing, and filled with all the latest bells and whistles, though. A simple site with four basic pages is sufficient—even one simple landing page is better than nothing at all. The four basic pages that are generally considered essential are a homepage, products and services page, about us page, and contact page.

Homepage

Your homepage is the first place your visitors will land when they click on your web address (URL). From your homepage, your prospect will immediately be able to see:
- who you are
- where you are
- what you do

This should be attractive, with good quality, relevant images, and also show your positioning statement—what you do that makes you better than your competitors. You also want to ensure it is easy to navigate around and back to from other pages in your site.

Products and Services Page

On this page your prospect will be able to see exactly what products and services you offer, and what problems they address. Think about what the most common questions your clients ask about what it is that you do, and answer those questions.

About Us Page

This is where you tell the story of your company—how and why it was founded—to give your prospect some insight into the *personality* of your company. You can express your company values, note any awards you have won or professional associations you are part of, and provide some customer testimonials from current and past clients. (If you have a number of testimonials, then making this a standout separate page is also a good idea, with case studies to support these.) This page is an integral part of telling your story, which will be covered in the next section of this book.

Contact Us Page

Your contact details should be prominently displayed, including your business hours, location, postal address, and links to your business social media pages. It is a good idea to put your phone number, if you have a 1800 number, and links to your social media pages on every page of your website, so your prospective clients can easily contact you from wherever they are on your website. It is current best practice to not add your mobile phone numbers or email addresses to your website as they are commonly scanned by spammers. However, a simple contact form with a captcha is easily added to most sites and still ensures visitors can quickly and efficiently get hold of you.

Setting Up Your Website

Website design is a dark art, and not for the fainthearted and inexperienced small business owner. There is a low barrier to entry into the website design industry (all you have to have is some knowledge of web tools), so there are inevitably lots of not-so-ethical people out there willing to talk to you in acronyms and geek-speak, take a whole lot of your money, and then produce a sub-standard site. I have heard far too many horror stories of businesses spending tens of thousands of dollars and finishing up with no site at all. Ask around amongst your business colleagues for recommendations, and make sure you check out some of their work before you proceed. If you have better-than-rudimentary knowledge and skills, you can try one of the outsourcing sites such as Upwork, 99designs, or Fiverr. Simple DIY website-building tools are starting to appear as well, where building a site is just drag and drop, and anyone with basic computer skills can develop a presentable website. Examples include Squarespace, Wix, and Weebly. Note, however, that there are disadvantages to using these tools instead of the traditional web platforms. For example, if you think you may want to move to another web hosting platform later on, you won't be able to shift your website, and you'll have to build it all over again.

WordPress is a platform that is used by more than 70% of businesses around the world and has been evolving since 2004. It's favoured by many for its simple efficiency and because it can be used with thousands of different plug-ins and themes for customisation. If you do wish to update it or change hosts at any time you don't need to throw the baby out with the bathwater and start fresh. You can simply move it and update it in a matter of hours.

Your Digital Footprint

I explained earlier in this section that, as well as checking out your website and email, your prospective customers will be checking out your overall digital footprint. They will Google you. Your responsibility is to make sure that what they see is congruent with your brand. Every picture you post and every social media comment—including comments on others' posts—are there for all to see. That includes your personal profiles as well as your business one. We, as small business owners, are indistinguishable from our companies in the eyes of our clients.

A "Like" or comment on an inappropriate image or a racist, political and sexist rant on Facebook, even the online groups you belong to, can rule you out of contention for further collaboration opportunities—and people are very quick to judge, it seems. Your big client will probably not want their brand associated with any controversy arising from your online behaviour. It still astounds me how many people do not get the power of social media. We recently advertised for a new consultant. One application looked excellent, until I checked his Facebook profile. Let's just say that he would not have been a good fit for our team.

This chapter is not intended to turn you into a digital genius. You will have to look elsewhere for that. What I wanted to emphasise to you is that your potential big customers will definitely be looking for you online, and what they find there will form a large part of their decision about whether to do business with you or not.

If you are not tech-savvy or willing to devise the best social media strategy for you or your business, it does pay to engage someone to at least get you looking smart, with professional copywriting. Then you can rest assured that your brand is presentable when potential customers search for you online.

Chapter 30
Getting Behind the Barriers

There are four main ways that small businesses get their foot in the door with their first big customer:

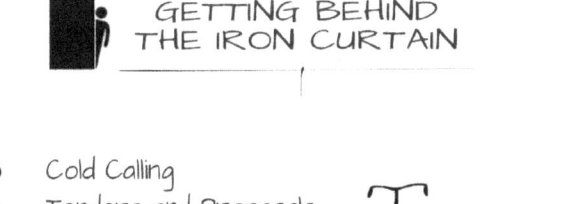

- Cold Calling
- Tenders and Proposals
- Contacts
- Networking

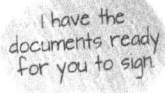

Contacts

In our own case, it was our personal contacts. My business partner had been working in the plantation industry for quite some years.

He and another colleague, Thomas, were concerned that adequate field training was not making its way down the management hierarchy to the on-ground teams—the ones actually doing and supervising the work. They decided to write a series of technical training manuals that were physically robust enough to be taken into the field. Effectively, the manuals were a set of safe work procedures for all the field tasks. Thomas was working for an international agribusiness organisation at the time, so that was our introduction to our very first contract. That organisation became the distributor for those manuals.

Years later, when the mining boom had started in Australia, our personal contacts helped us again. That introduction came from a landholder whose property adjoined a coal mining site. The mining company was required to monitor groundwater levels, in case the mining operations disrupted any groundwater aquifers. We had worked for this property owner in the past, and had a good relationship with him and his family. When it came to having his groundwater tested, he insisted that our local company do the monitoring. He felt that we were local, accountable, and trustworthy. We were employed to do the work. That small contract led to more work on-site, and we have been supplying that site with environmental monitoring services continuously since then.

Your peer networks are your very best ally. Asking someone who both knows and trusts you to put you in contact with your preferred target is gold. Of course, you must go about this carefully so as not to upset either your contact or your target, and this is an entire field of specialisation. I have included resources gleaned from some of my colleagues who are experts in this area on the *Small Company, Big Business* website so you can learn about what to do and what *not to do*.

Tenders

Online tender databases are being used more often by large corporations, and you need to have knowledge of how to use these as part of your arsenal for breaking into big companies. In fact some companies will only take on suppliers through their online tendering site. More and more big organisations, and government departments, are turning to the use of online tendering or online expressions of interest as a means of recruiting suppliers.

For some big companies, tenders are the only way in. There are several large online tender databases that big corporations use such as ICN Gateway. ICN Gateway is an independent organisation, financially supported by all Australian governments (federal, state, and territory) as well as the New Zealand government. *All* potential suppliers can lodge their profile and capabilities on the ICN website, using keywords to indicate their areas of interest; this is not just limited to mining companies. Potential suppliers will then be notified by email when an opportunity arises in their area of expertise.

Project proponents can also search the ICN database for suppliers with a particular expertise, and approach them directly.

Corporations will often list a Tier 1 opportunity first, and then subsequent Tier 2, 3, or 4 opportunities as they arise.

Another potential use of the ICN Gateway is to use it to see which companies have been awarded the Tier 1 contracts for major projects. Then you can approach those Tier 1 contractors directly.

Some companies prefer to use their own proprietary databases, for example QGC, Bechtel. Western Australia, where construction projects are typically multi-billion dollar affairs.

Another option is to partner with a local economic development agency or Chamber of Commerce in order to reach potential suppliers. This model is an ideal opportunity for small businesses to get close to their intended large company targets.

Paying attention to the online databases needs to become one of the regular weekly administration tasks undertaken by every small supplier. It's time consuming, and you may not be successful in winning contracts from the tender sites but, like the Gold Lotto, if you don't have a ticket, you certainly won't win.

When you sign up to the online tender databases you will generally have to upload your:

- capability statement, outlining your products and services and your experience
- three or more years of financial statements
- documentary evidence of your occupational health and safety system
- environmental and quality systems
- insurance documents

It is important that these documents be updated regularly, to ensure that they are current.

Never prepared a Tender before? Access the "Introduction to Tendering" online training on my website. Details are on page 283.

Networking

I can feel many of you cringing from here at the very thought of going to a networking event. At least 50% of small business owners say that they don't like networking, and that it makes them feel uncomfortable. It is said that many people would prefer death to speaking in public, and attending a networking event to talk to strangers is just as bad.

As with most things you have to do in small business, there's a right and a wrong way to go about networking. Arriving with a fist full of business cards and pushing them on everyone in the room is the wrong way. Turning a conversation into a sales pitch is also on the naughty list. Instead, you should introduce yourself with your elevator pitch—a short summary of who you are, what you do, and the products/services you provide—which, of course, you will have practiced. If there is to be a sales conversation, follow up after the event.

There are some fantastic books about networking and relationship development for business that are well worth reading, including Lindsay Adams' *The DNA of Business Relationships*. But here's my top three pieces of advice to consider when faced with heading out to your next business event.

Go prepared

The number one rule of networking is **be helpful**. It's not all about you. You can help yourself do this by doing some research beforehand. Are these regular events? Who is hosting the event? Who is likely to be attending? Who will be there that you would like to meet? What can you find out about your networking target? By going to the event prepared, you will avoid a feeling of overwhelm when you walk into the crowd.

Another way you can be helpful is to make introductions. Help others make connections with a simple, "I think Brian, who I met earlier, would be a good contact for you. Let me introduce you." If a mutually beneficial connection is made, both parties will remember the good deed you did for them.

Keep moving

This is something that I struggle with at times. I get into an absolutely fascinating conversation with someone, and before I know it, the event is over and I've only met one person in the whole room. Be brave enough to move on; you won't offend anyone. After all, it is a networking event. A simple comment such as, "It's been great meeting you, and I'll definitely send through that information you asked for. I just need to catch up with a few more people before they disappear," is all that is needed.

However, if you are at an event where you're seated for a meal, it can be great to do a card swap (either the old-fashioned way or with a smartphone app) with others at your table and a quick mention of following up at another time with those you don't get to further engage with. If you do that, then aim for that to happen within 24 hours, so your face is still fresh in their minds.

Follow up

Once you arrive home from the networking event, take a few minutes to empty all those business cards from your pockets. If necessary, make some notes about your new contacts so you don't forget what you talked about, or what they requested from you. You will retain 90% of what you heard if you do this immediately. The longer you wait, the more you will forget.

This is also your opportunity to make connections via your social media accounts, particularly LinkedIn. That's where your potential customers will be, and the wider your network is, the better chance there is that you will be able to interact with them. Reach out with a simple message reminding them where they met you and what you discussed. If you promised to send them anything (a document, the name of a contact, some information, etc.), do it. Unless you have agreed at the networking event, it's still not time to launch into a sales pitch. Just because you met someone, that doesn't mean they automatically want to buy something from you. As Lindsay Adams says, "It's a bit like dating. You are unlikely to propose on a first date or even the second or third. You need to get to know each other a little better before calling it a 'relationship'."

Networking is a long game, not for short-term results. By being a polite, helpful networker, you will slowly build an impressive network of contacts who know you can add value to either themselves or someone they know.

In fact, when I was interviewing business owners for this book, every single person told me at least one story about getting work through somebody who knew somebody who knew somebody. The truth is that in many cases you won't get work at all unless you know somebody who knows somebody who knows somebody.

Chapter 31
Partnerships

Partnerships and alliances are the secret weapons of any business—small, medium or large. They allow us leverage to appear bigger than we really are, and offer skills, products, and services that we don't have ourselves. But like many weapons, they are only useful if managed correctly. I mentioned earlier in this book about the different levels of business skills. I understand that many small business owners view their "business baby" with almost the same level of pride and protection as their real-life children. The prospect of sharing your business with someone else can be difficult to overcome, and so forming successful partnerships requires mature thinking. Nevertheless, strategic partnerships are becoming a vital element of many small business operations in a modern globalised world.

In this chapter I will give you some guidelines for creating successful, win-win partnerships, as well as showing you the enormous benefits you can achieve if you form partnerships successfully.

What Is a Partnership?

Partnership is one of those words that has a multitude of meanings, so the first thing to do is make sure both parties to a new partnership know what the other means. First, there is a legal meaning of partnership. A partnership is one legal structure for a business entity, as are sole trader and specific company structures. However, this strict legal definition is not what I am referring to in this chapter.

In my experience, there are three levels of business partnership, differentiated by the degree of integration between the two parties: collaborative partnerships, strategic partnerships, and joint ventures.

Collaborative partnerships

This is where two parties get together for the purpose of promoting each other's businesses. Think celebrities and perfume companies, or supermarkets and celebrity chefs. The idea is that, together, your businesses can do more than you both could individually. This may be as simple as promoting your partner's (complementary) product to your existing database, or doing a joint promotion. Collaborative partnerships are easy to form, generally have no legal structure around them, and can generate some quick wins for both parties. The two parties remain as completely separate businesses, and there is no involvement by each party in the other's company.

Strategic partnerships

This is what most people think of when they consider the concept of partnerships. Strategic partnerships involve a closer degree of cooperation between the parties, and usually have a written agreement outlining the roles and responsibilities of each. Strategic partners are looking to leverage each other's brand and assets to grow revenue and their combined markets. They may look at how to cut costs together. Under this arrangement, the partners will be looking at the internal workings of the other party a bit more. They will get to know each other better, so that each can represent the other in their marketing materials and conversations.

Our consultancy business has several strategic partnerships with other small businesses. One advantage of these has been the ability to bid on projects that would otherwise not be available. For example, if a project requires some skills that we don't have in-house, we can call on one of our trusted strategic partners to supply those skills. **We have already agreed how we will arrange our commercial relationship**, so the client receives a seamless experience, and both of us earn revenue that neither of us would have had access to without our pre-arranged strategic partnership.

Having our strategic partnerships well mapped out similarly means that we can work under their banner and access projects that would otherwise be closed to us. Our partners also supply us with pre-qualified leads, as we do in reverse.

Another example is where some large companies will offer work only to their select group of suppliers, such as within the medical industry—for example, within a medical clinic, doctors and midwives, chiropractors, and psychologists may have firm agreements in place to recommend each other almost exclusively, not only because of their combined location, but due to the strategic partnerships between their separate businesses.

So you can see that forming a strategic partnership is a lot more than just an exchange of money or a friendly referral relationship. Partnerships can become one of the core assets of your business.

Joint ventures

Joint ventures take the partner relationship further again. At this stage, you are getting serious and creating a formal relationship. Think of it like getting married. Usually there will be a separate legal entity created, jointly owned by the partners (there may be more than just two), with all the partners sharing the costs. A word of caution here: just as you wouldn't get married as soon as you meet a potential life partner (silly TV reality shows excepted), you should not jump into a joint venture without due consideration. If you are approached out of the blue to form a joint venture, your business BS detector should be tuned to the highest sensitivity level. Your suitor may be looking to you as their lifeline to solve their own internal issues such as a cash flow, or looming reputation or qualifications issues.

How Can Partnerships Help?

After working with small businesses for many years, and having established several strategic partnerships myself, I have identified three great reasons why you should step outside your comfort zone, and partner up.

1. New customers, new market segments.

A carefully chosen strategic partner can introduce you to a whole new set of customers. 57% of business owners say they have formed partnerships to find new customers.[26] Those new customers may even be in another state, or even overseas. If the partners provide complementary products or services, joining together means that everyone can pitch to new customers with a combined offering. This has been a particularly successful strategy for my company.

2. Increased revenue/decreased costs.

Attracting new customers will almost certainly increase your revenue. A strategic alliance can also mean increased sales to existing clients—your combined offering may solve a customer's problem that you couldn't solve individually. Partnerships can also help reduce costs by sharing fixed costs amongst the partners, and increase profits by enhancing productivity. Perhaps you can also achieve some economies of scale as

---

26   breezy.io. (n.d.). *104 Stats You Never Knew About Strategic Partnerships | Breezy*. [online] Available at: https://breezy.io/blog/strategic-partnership-stats.

your production increases to serve your new customers. Importantly, partnerships can also reduce financial risk by sharing financial commitments (and associated risks). In addition, having a regular partner to work with increases efficiency, as you don't have to source and qualify a new supplier every time you need a particular service.

3. Making friends with big companies.

Solving big companies' problems together with your strategic partner can be especially valuable. To enlist a new supplier, big companies have to complete mountains of paperwork. So, if your partnership can solve a big company's problems without them having to enlist another supplier, those big company contacts will breathe a sigh of relief.

What Can Partnerships Do for You?

Keep your client close to you

Like a jealous lover, you need to keep your big company contact close. Provide them with all (or as much as you can) of what they need to make them look good and they won't go looking elsewhere.

Strategic alliances, collaborative partnerships, and joint ventures can give your small business a real advantage in the eyes of your target big buyers. But like any long-term relationship, it is important to stop, think, and prepare before taking the leap to prevent heartache later.

Offer additional products and services

You offer the deep knowledge that only a lifetime of practice can give. An alliance brings the skills of other specialists like you to your client without them having to:
- spend the time to go searching themselves
- deal with more than one contractor—big companies hate dealing with multiple contractors

Having partners with complementary skills and/or products allows a small business to extend their offering. I have seen this work particularly well with professional service providers, where specialists with niche skills come together to provide a service that competes very effectively with their bigger competitors.

Access new technologies and skills
Sharing resources gives a small business access to the expertise, experience, and knowledge of all the other partners. Two (or more) heads are better than one, and someone else's experience and perspective can be invaluable in solving a client's problems. Partnerships can give your small business access to technology that it would otherwise be impossible (or extremely expensive) to acquire yourself.

Shared resources
Big companies have access to a lot more resources than small businesses, but partnerships allow us to compete by combining the tools, personnel, and skills that we do have. A successful partnership can help all parties by sharing many business functions such as joint marketing and advertising, product development, or even HR.

Business resilience

Having partners can help your business ride out some tough times. For example, research from the University of Queensland[27] has shown that connectedness—the ability to actively cultivate and maintain business network partnerships—is one of the four key factors that have helped successful small businesses survive the end of the resources boom.

In the words of one business owner I interviewed for this book: "*Then there is this important thing that you won't get anywhere without and that's your network.*"

I can personally attest to the truth of this benefit. As the resources boom went bust, purchase orders that had already been issued to us and resourced disappeared like a snowflake in Cairns in January. It was our consultancy company's partners that gave us access to alternative markets that allowed us to keep trading profitably, albeit at a reduced turnover.

Many businesses discovered the value of solid networks and partnerships during the COVID-19 pandemic era of 2020 to 2022. These provided support when rapid changes had to be made in order to survive. Keep in mind too that some 60–70% of corporate alliances fail, so next I will share what I have learned about how to make your partnership one of the successful ones.

How to Make a Successful Partnership

Here are six key areas for developing a partnership that works well.

---

27   Ana Maria Esteves, Mary Anne Barclay, Daniel Samson, and David Brereton, *Local SME Participation in the Supply Chains of Australian Mining, Oil and Gas Companies* (Brisbane: Centre for Social Responsibility in Mining, University of Queensland, 2009).

1. Have a clearly defined purpose

The purpose of the collaboration must be written down, clear, and without ambiguity. Like written goals, a clear statement that is agreed upon up-front prevents "scope creep" and misunderstandings. You can't just be coming together for a drink on Friday afternoons. There has to be a purpose to the collaboration with established communication plans for ensuring this is understood and maintained for the benefit of all involved.

2. A common issue or problem

Collaborating is hard, and business owners will solve a problem themselves if they can. But if they can't, self-interest will drive them to seek an alternative. If someone else shares the same pain, it is in both parties' interest to collaborate to find a solution. The reward for collaborating must be greater than the discomfort of giving up some of your own independence. Approaching all aspects of this partnership must be a win/win for everyone.

3. Hope for the future

One of my business mentors put it this way: *"The collaboration has to be a means to an end, not an end in itself." When you set off on a* partnership journey in response to an initial problem, you really don't know where it's going to end. The alliance may open up a whole set of unanticipated opportunities. You have to be prepared to get on the train together, trust each other, and keep going. And it bears repeating here, you must all have a win/win attitude with good communication strategies.

4. The right people with authority

I have seen a lot of time and money wasted on partnership negotiations, only to have the entire venture scrapped by someone with more decision-making authority. Make sure that the person setting out to create the alliance in the first place has the authority, including the **financial and sign-off authority**, to do so.

5. Formal documentation

As divorce lawyers like to say, "Nothing says 'I love you' like a contract." Have a short document that contains the partnership's clearly defined purpose, how the alliance will work and, **most importantly, a dispute resolution clause. If you do this up front, in most cases it will go into the bottom drawer of your desk and never see the light of day again. What's important is that the** document exists, setting out the structure of the relationship in the first place, should you ever need to refer to it. Of course, as your partnership progresses from collaboration (dating), through strategic partnership (engaged) to joint venture (marriage), the level of documentation will increase.

6. Don't be precious

As a small business owner, your company is perhaps your whole life's work. The concept of sharing, and sharing unconditionally, may be difficult to digest, but it's absolutely vital to a successful partnership. The big question, and the critical success factor for all partnerships is "What can I do for you?", not "What can you do for me?"

The critical success factor for all partnerships is "What can I do for you?", not "What can you do for me?"

Look Out for Trigger Events

An excellent opportunity to introduce yourself to a prospective new client is to watch the news for trigger events, and offer your valuable services to a company that finds itself in need of them.

One of the most profitable and long-term projects our consultancy ever completed was following such a trigger event. An environmental incident had occurred and made the newspapers. We knew that we had exactly the right skill set and expertise to help this company out of what was proving to be an environmental and public relations nightmare. The company had no idea that we existed, so we approached them with a plan to help. Despite some initial reluctance on their part about engaging a small supplier, we worked together for months to rectify the problem.

Trigger events don't have to be someone else's misfortune, although many are. Budget announcements and elections are prime times for picking up opportunities. I mentioned in Chapter 21 about the Australian Government plan to install insulation in household ceilings throughout the country. That announcement meant an immediate upturn in business for insulation manufacturers and installers for those who were quick off the mark. The program did end badly, but it is an excellent example of a trigger event that some suppliers immediately capitalised on at the time.

Anniversaries or good news stories are also an opportunity to reach out to your prospective customers. If they have recently won an award, or been successful in winning a big contract, that's the time for you to send them a congratulatory message and an introduction as to how your company could add value to their new opportunity.

Supply to a Supplier

Another excellent way to let your target client know that you exist is by becoming a supplier to one of their suppliers. Back in Section 1, I introduced the concept of a supply chain. If you are providing excellent service to a Tier 2 company, your chances of being noticed by your main target are increased. For example, if you prepare a report for your Tier 2 customer that eventually makes it onto the desk of someone of influence in the Tier 1 target, you are suddenly on their radar.

SECTION 6
TELL YOUR STORY

Now that you have everything else in place to go and catch your big client, the last step is to convince them that they really, really need you. You have to tell them your story.

When working with clients, this is one of the points on which I get a significant amount of resistance to my suggestions—and reluctance to try something different. "Storytelling," they say, "is for children and fairy tales. It has no place in business, especially when I'm trying to talk to a big company or a government department."

Nothing could be further from the truth. This is the power of connecting with emotions, and the most powerful way to do that in business is through storytelling.

Chapter 32
The Importance of Storytelling

We often forget that B2B (business-to-business) selling is really just H2H (human-to-human) selling, and humans love stories. Our ancestors have been telling and listening to stories for millennia, so we've become used to it. In fact, we love hearing stories—storytelling triggers strong neurological responses in our brains. A happy ending to a story triggers the release of dopamine, the "feel good" chemical. So, by providing a story with a happy ending (such as a successful case study where you solved a tricky problem for another client, or the story of how your business started and grew to be the success it is today), you are actually providing your prospective client with an enjoyable dopamine hit.

Consider this: how long is it since you saw something in a shop/catalogue/online that you absolutely fell in love with, but your rational brain knew you definitely did not need it? I know it has happened to me, often. Your rational being is perfectly sensible, and is screaming at you to walk away. But your emotions are pulling you the other way. "You love it, you really have to have it!" If (when) you hand over your credit card, your rational brain will immediately begin coming up with perfectly rational reasons for your acting the way you did. "The old car was getting a few too many kilometres up and would probably start breaking down soon," or "I can wear that if I have an unexpected formal dinner to attend." You know this feeling, and you know you've done it.

At the point of decision making, emotions rule. Even if we like to think we are making perfectly rational decisions, none of us can completely escape the influence of emotions. What you are doing is using your stories to create an emotional climate that is conducive to your potential client choosing in your favour.

But does storytelling have a place in formal business documents like project proposals and tenders?

The answer is a resounding yes. Your story is what differentiates you from your competitors, but many small business owners go out of their way to tell their target audience how they are exactly the same as their competitors. As an example, take a minute now and search a few accountancy firms' websites. They will all tell you that they're different, and then populate the rest of their website telling how they do tax returns, financial planning, and will organise your lease finance. What a surprise. Fancy an accountant doing tax returns and financial planning! Then there is the ever popular "We offer a wide range of quality services."

What your big new customer needs to know is not **how** they can work with you, but **why** they should work with you—and that is where your story is important. What drives your company? Where have you come from? Where are you going?

This can be hard at first if you are used to traditional marketing, and it's often hard to dispassionately examine your own business to see what it is that makes you different. Ask your existing customers why they chose you, and what it is that keeps them coming back. You may be surprised at the answers you get.

Apart from making an emotional connection with your customer and helping them to like you more (and we like people we understand better than those we don't), storytelling serves another vital function in making yourself known. It tells your customer what you are capable of helping them with. I know, that sounds so basic as to be silly, but surprisingly, there is a huge gap between sellers and buyers. Two-thirds of buyers (i.e., your potential customers) report that they don't know all the services their suppliers can offer.[28] Why would they say this when you've told them already?

Put yourself in the customer's shoes. How much notice do you take of cars advertisements on the TV? My answer is, "Most of the time, absolutely none." However, when our daughter was in the market for her very first car, I suddenly became very interested. Which brand has the highest safety rating? Which costs the least to run? How much does each model cost? And so it went. She bought a great car, and I quickly reverted to my usual state of completely ignoring car ads. Your customer is the same. When they are trying to solve a particular problem with your product or service, they won't be tuned into all the other things you can do. Even if you tell them, chances are that it will pass through their conscious brain and straight out the other side. You need to continually remind them of your capabilities, and telling stories such as successful case studies is an excellent way to do just that.

Over half your potential buyers report that they would like to purchase more services from their existing sellers.[29] By not constantly reminding them of your offerings, you are effectively leaving easy money on the table.

Hopefully, by now, I've convinced you of the power, and indeed

---

28   Hinge Research Institute, *How Buyers Buy*, 2013, https://hingemarketing.com/library/article/how_buyers_buy_professional_services_buyers_study.
29   Hinge Research Institute, *How Buyers Buy*, 2013, https://hingemarketing.com/library/article/how_buyers_buy_professional_services_buyers_study.

the necessity, of storytelling in business. It will probably feel odd at first, but with practice, weaving stories into your marketing will become a natural part of the way you do business.

The next question to be answered is where do we tell these stories? How do you get the opportunity to tell your prospective big customers about your business, and how you can solve their problems?

Apart from your social media platforms, there are a number of opportunities to do this. The first one I want to tell you about is a document that you may not have even heard about before—a capability statement.

Chapter 33
Capability Statements

What Is a Capability Statement?

A *capability statement* is a cross between a company brochure and a business card on steroids. In short, it tells your prospective client exactly what you and your company are capable of doing—your **capabilities**. On occasion, you will see them referred to as a business profile or even as corporate credentials.

Think of it as your **company's resume**, telling your prospective client how you will solve their particular problem.

> **In the real world ...**
> Twice in the same week, I received panicked phone calls from two different small business owners. This in itself was not new, as I am often sourced for helpful advice, but in both cases, they had been asked by a potential large client (a mining company in one case, and a government department in the other) for a capability statement.
> One of the business owners actually knew what one
> >>

was but had no clue how to prepare one or what should be in it.

The second person told me that they had no option but to endure the uncomfortable silence that ensued. They had no idea what a capability statement was, so they couldn't even answer yes or no. This is not a good look for a small business owner trying their best to pitch to a very large prospective client.

Like a good resume, you will need to tailor your capability statement to the individual client you are trying to attract. In each one you will address that client's particular issues, and how they will benefit from engaging your company. If you serve several market segments, prepare a separate capability statement for each. For example, one of my own companies provides services to both the agriculture and mining industries. These are two very different markets, so a different capability statement is appropriate for each of them.

You need to clearly convey four things in your capability statement:

1. Capabilities: What are your competencies? What is it that you do? What products or services do you supply? What areas do you serve? What size projects can you undertake?
2. Differentiators: What makes you different from your competitors? Why should they choose you? Do you have any special licences, patents, equipment, or software? What is your value proposition?
3. Company details: Details about your company such as your contact details, company structure, ABN, insurances and such.
4. Experience: What experience have you had doing similar work to that which you are pitching to your big client? Who can your prospective client contact as a referee?

Four Excellent Reasons to Have a Capability Statement

1. Because you have to
When applying for tenders (I'll talk about tenders later in this section), you will often have to submit your capability statement. In fact, for many companies this is a must, and not having one will rule you out of contention at the first hurdle.

2. Communication
A capability statement is a powerful communication tool. In the world of big business and centralised procurement, it can be hard to make your message heard, and it lets your prospective clients know the facts about your company so they can make initial decisions about engaging with you.

3. Building trust
First impressions are important and a well prepared and informative capability statement is therefore a brilliant strategic marketing tool. It is often the first touch point that starts the process of building trust between your two companies. It may even contain some commercially sensitive information that has been prepared especially for a particular prospect, which further engenders a level of trust in your willingness to be transparent and to "get on board" with what's required.

4. Differentiation
Your capability statement is the ideal tool to reinforce your brand and your value proposition. This is your opportunity to tell your prospective customers exactly why they should engage you rather than your competition.

The Golden Rule: Make It Look Good

Your capability statement should be a visually attractive document, so engage a designer if your skills don't go beyond Microsoft Word. High quality images and no spelling errors are compulsory.

What to Put in a Capability Statement

Starting your first capability statement from scratch can be quite daunting, so to help you along the way, there is a template available on the resources section of the Small Company Big Business website which you'll find a link to on page 281.

This is the first document where you have an opportunity to tell your story. Please, don't do the "once upon a time" version in your capability statement, but you do need to weave some of your company's story and personality into the document. This will probably mean that you need to collaborate with a professional writer (as well as a graphic designer), but believe me, the investment will be well worth it.

Chapter 34
Bids, Tenders, Proposals—What?

Now that you have your company capability statement under way, let's turn our attention to other places where you have the opportunity to tell your story, and attract the attention of your potential customers—proposals and tenders.

But first you need to understand some of the language. Like most professions, the procurement profession has created an entire language and terminology of its own. They speak in acronyms and use words that other human beings don't understand. In fact, there are so many acronyms that seem to be interchangeable, it often seems that the big company procurement department themselves don't know what they should be using.

This book is not going to be a dictionary of procurement terminology, but there are two commonly used terms that it is worthwhile understanding the difference between: tenders and proposals .

What Is a Tender?

The majority of big companies, government departments and councils find the goods and services they need by using a process called ***tendering***, where everyone (theoretically) has an equal opportunity to participate. There are two main steps in the tendering process:

1. A buyer specifies what goods and/or services they need, and then asks potential suppliers to submit a response by a set date, outlining how they will meet the requirements, and how much their solution will cost. The buyer issues a request for tender (RFT).
2. The buyer then chooses its preferred supplier from all the responses received, based on price, delivery terms, value, delivery times, and a host of other possible criteria.

Sadly, too many small business owners believe that tendering is only for the big guys, and stay away.

The tender process is used when the buyer is sure (or at least they think they are sure) about *exactly* what they want. The tender documents will contain detailed specifications of what goods or services are required, and any standards or qualifications that have to be met. In short, the scope of works and the deliverables expected will be quite clear and very specific.

Tender responses are required to be in a defined format. You will be given a number of forms and templates, and your response must be made in those documents. You must tell your story in your responses to the questions on the supplied documents. It's not all bad news, though. You should always add a cover letter, and usually include an executive summary as well. You can use these two components of your response to give a "free-form" version of why your tender submission should be accepted.

When replying to a tender, you must tell your story within your answers on the documents supplied.

In the real world ...

The Rockhampton Regional Council is looking for a contractor to transport waste. Obviously, the council has an already established waste transfer facility (formerly known as a dump), and waste collection rounds. The new contractor will therefore have to fit in around these already-established routines and equipment.

1 SCOPE OF WORKS

1.1.1   *ABC Regional is seeking tender submissions from suitably qualified contractors for providing a service for transferring uncompacted municipal solid waste from the Lakes Creek Road Waste Transfer Station to the active working face on the landfill.*

1.1.2   *Typically, the waste transfer station may receive 20 tonnes of waste per day. This daily tonnage may vary from 10–15 tonnes on weekends to 25–30 tonnes on weekdays.*

1.1.3   *Waste transfer services are required six (6) days per week, Monday to Saturday. Typical estimates around the number of services, waste transfers and preferred transfer times are presented in Table 1.*

Table 1: Waste Transfer Service Requirements

Day	Number of Services	No. of Transfers	Preferred Transfer Times
Monday	2 services	3–5	9a.m. and 2p.m.
Tuesday	1 service	2–3	2p.m.
Wednesday	1 service	2–3	2p.m.
Thursday	1 service	2–3	2p.m.
Friday	1 service	2–3	2p.m.
Saturday	1 service	2–3	2p.m.

>>

1.1.4 *Note that two (2) services are required each Monday. The 9 a.m. service is to largely clear Sunday's waste, while the 2 p.m. service is to largely clear Monday's waste.*

1.1.5 *The number of services and transfers required per service are estimates only and may vary from time to time.*

1.1.6 *In the event the contractor is unable to provide the required services in accordance with Table 1, prior approval must be provided by Council.*

1.1.7 *Tenderers are to submit their service fee per waste transfer along with their proposed vehicle and bin configuration in (Schedule 2).*

1.1.8 *Tenderers are to provide a brief description of their proposed waste transfer methods including back-up options and strategies for minimising downtime in (Schedule 3).*

2 WASTE TRANSFER VEHICLE SPECIFICATION

2.1.1 *The waste transfer bin and vehicle must fit the dimensions of the waste transfer station drop-pit to minimise waste spillage. The dimensions of the waste transfer station drop-pit are provided below:*
a) Length – 13.5 m
b) Width – 2.5 m
c) Height (from the ground level) – 4.55 m

2.1.2 *The following bin and vehicle configuration is required:*

$30m^3$ roll-on roll-off (RORO) bin and a RORO truck with an appropriate load capacity.

Notice how the scope of works is very specific. The services must be provided a prescribed number of times on prescribed days, and the waste transfer vehicle must be a "30m³ roll-on roll-off (RORO) bin and a RORO truck with an appropriate load capacity", a very specific requirement.

Alternative Tenders

Sometimes, however, you may have an even better way of complying with the buyer's requirements. Let's assume that your extremely innovative small business has invented a waste transfer robot that will do the same job, only faster and cheaper. Of course, you would love to present your new robot to the council for this particular project, as you would have a real competitive advantage. This will be an ***alternative tender***.

The rules are that, in this situation, you must submit a ***conforming tender***. That is, you must submit a tender to supply the waste transfer truck, **exactly** in accordance with the scope of works and all the other tender conditions. Then, you also submit your ***alternative***

tender, which tells them all about your new robot.

A typical alternative tender clause will look something like this:

> *Where a tenderer seeks to vary the tender criteria referred to in clause 8.1.3, the tenderer may, subject to this clause, in addition to any conforming tender submitted, also submit an alternative tender clearly marked as "alternative tender". An alternative tender may only be submitted if the tenderer has also submitted a conforming tender. The alternative tender must clearly describe the extent to which the tender criteria are proposed to be varied by, amongst other things, completing the statement of additions and variations found in tender Schedule 2.*
>
> *8.2.2 An alternative tender is not a conforming tender.*
>
> *8.2.3 Council may, but is not bound to, consider or accept any alternative tender or non-conforming tender.*

Note that you must submit your conforming tender *as well*, and that the council does not have to consider your alternative tender if it doesn't want to. Maybe waste robots are just a bit too revolutionary for them just at the moment.

Even if the tender documents don't mention alternative tenders, don't be put off from presenting your robot solution. In the first instance, ask the tender contact (I'll talk about this later) about how to submit your alternative solution.

Proposals

While the terms "tender" and "proposal" are often used interchangeably, there is a slight difference between the two. As we saw, when a buyer issues a tender, they are quite certain about the exact scope of works, and your reply must be submitted in the required format.

Sometimes, however, a buyer has a problem that they're not certain how to solve. So, the ***request for proposal (RFP)*** will outline the problem and the desired outcome, and the potential suppliers are invited to come up with a solution. In other words, the RFP concentrates on the end, not the means.

> **In the real world ...**
> *Request for Proposal (RFP)*
> *The Central Highlands Development Corporation (CHDC) and Central Highlands Regional Council (CHRC) are seeking to engage the services of a suitably qualified contractor with experience in economics, technology, and project management and planning. This tender is to provide two bodies of work including:*
> 1. *A detailed digital and telecommunications audit to identify what infrastructure/enablers exists at present and what the opportunities are;*
> 2. *A plan to provide clear identification of what actions need to be progressed to address identified deficiencies or opportunities, while considering the opportunities of current and future growth and demand.*
>
> *OR*
>
> *To conduct two bodies of work including a digital and telecommunications audit that identifies what infrastructure/enablers exist and articulate in a plan what the opportunities are and actions that need to take place over the short and long term. [Both taken from the same RFP.]*

Notice how the scope of works in this RFP is a lot less specific than in the tender case study, and the respondents will be able to propose their own unique approach to conducting the project. For example, the successful applicant may conduct a desktop audit, followed up by site visits to inspect the communications infrastructure, or they may stop at the desktop audit and base the remainder of the project on just the desktop audit information.

Your response to an RFP[30] is not necessarily constrained by specified forms and documents to complete, although there may be some. To present your unique solution, you have complete freedom in how your response is structured.

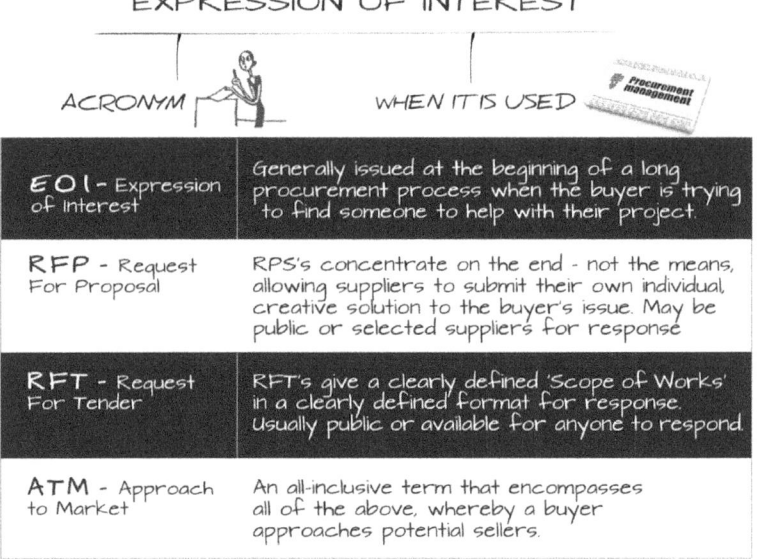

This is by no means an exhaustive list of the acronyms used in the language of procurement, but these are commonly used terms that you will encounter most often.

---

30 In Section 5, I emphasised the importance of building your brand and company profile. Part of your work in building your profile with your brand, your website, networking, forming partnerships, etc., is to ensure that you are one of the recipients of the request for proposals. If they don't know about you, you certainly won't be on the list.

Chapter 35

Tenders and Proposals—How They Work and Where to Find Them

Now that you know the difference between tenders and proposals, you need to know:
- where to look for tenders and proposals that you can reply to
- how to write tenders and proposals that win

So, where do you start looking? Do your target customers even consider your small business a potential supplier? What sort of work could you do for them?

The Not-So-Secret Stash of Potential Leads

Fortunately, there is a place where you can go to find the answer to all of these questions and more. Surprisingly though, most small businesses never go there.

That place is **online tender sites**. At this point, I want to assure you again that tenders are most definitely not reserved just for big businesses, and that you could be missing out on huge opportunities by ignoring the tender process. I do understand though if you are initially reluctant to dip your toe into this new pool of marketing techniques. Quite frankly, tenders used to scare me to death, but since I learned how to search for them and write good submissions, they have become an integral part of my marketing mix.

Government tenders

All levels of government (local, state and national, in Australia and New Zealand) advertise their tenders on purpose-built websites. While these are online, they are unfortunately not all in the same place. For each of these sites, you will have to create your supplier profile and create a login username and password. Once you are logged in to the sites, you can specify what type of tenders you are interested in, and set up email alerts to let you know when something of interest is listed. Some sites even list their forward procurement plans—tenders that will be coming up, but are not yet open for submissions. Even better, State Governments are targeting SMEs for increasing amounts of their procurement spending – up to 50% in the case of Tasmania.

For Queensland companies who don't yet have experience with tendering, a good place to start is at the local government level because the prequalification requirements are often less stringent. Many councils also give a hand-up to local companies by implementing a "local buy" policy.

There is a list of government tender websites in the resources section of the Small Company, Big Business website.

Private sector tenders

Non-government tenders are even more spread out across the internet. Most of these will be covered by the commercial tender sites if you are willing to pay the required fee. Otherwise, it's a case of some intense Google searching and some telephone time. Many large companies have their own tender portals on their website, so check out your target company's site for opportunities. Phone your local council to find out their tendering arrangements. Major infrastructure projects (such as for the Commonwealth Games) can be found on the ICN Gateway.

Do you have to search every single site?

If continually searching all these websites seems to be way too much work, you're probably right. There are some short-cuts available, though. Each of these sites allows you to set up email alerts when tenders that you may be interested in are posted. You will still have to visit all the different sites to check out the alerts.

If you are prepared to spend a bit of money out of your marketing budget, you could consider using one of the commercial tender portals. These websites are commercial businesses that scan all the available government sites, as well as private sector and international sites, newspapers, government gazettes, journals, and just about every other conceivable place where a tender might be published. Once you set up your profile, you will be alerted to any opportunity. Of course, there is a fee for this service, but they will certainly save you time and effort.

Not All Tenders Are Listed Online

Then there are many tenders that are not advertised online at all. They may be *restricted tenders*, where only a few suppliers are invited, or *direct sourcing* where just one pre-qualified supplier is contacted.

So, how do you access these tenders? The answer is—not easily. Of the small business owners I spoke to, 73% tell me that getting on the radar of their potential big clients so that they even get the opportunity to tender is their number one hurdle. The only solution to this challenge is devoting time and energy to some power networking—both in person and on LinkedIn—to raise your company profile. Establishing relationships is key, but it does require patience.

Proposals — You Have to Get on the List

While some RFPs are listed on the tender sites mentioned, the majority are sent to an already selected list of potential suppliers. These companies may have been identified through an earlier call for suppliers to tender to be on a pre-qualified list. The RFP will only be sent to those whom the buyer already knows have the capability, skill, qualifications, and systems to complete the work.

In other cases, the buyer's procurement team will only send the RFP to the potential suppliers that it is aware of—those who have supplied to them previously, and others that have come to their attention as a potential supplier. Now you can see the importance of building your company profile that we discussed in Section 5. If they don't know you exist, they certainly won't be asking you for a proposal.

If you are new to the Tendering process, it can be quite overwhelming. I remember clearly trying to prepare our first mining company tender. It was for BHP. Years later, I found a paper copy of it in a store room. Totally cringeworthy! The BHP people must have had a good old laugh. To save you the same fate, I have an "Introduction to Tendering" short, online course on my website. Details are on page 283.

Chapter 36
Start Local

Local Content Policies

One of the best avenues into the supply chain of a large company or a government department is through a ***local buying*** or ***local content policy***.

We looked earlier at the concept of a social licence to operate, and corporate social responsibility. Large companies and governments will purchase a certain amount of their goods and services from local businesses in order to boost local economies, foster local skills development, and engender goodwill—in other words, to earn their social licence to operate and fulfil their corporate social responsibility obligations.

Many industries have their own local content policies, and these can vary widely in what they cover, and what they consider "local". For example, the Australian state of Queensland has a Queensland Charter for Local Content, which defines local industries as "Australian or New Zealand small and medium-sized enterprises (SMEs)."[31] For

---

31   Department of State Development, Infrastructure, Local Government and Planning, *Queensland Charter for Local Content: Best Practice Guidelines for Agencies June 2021* (Brisbane: Queensland Government, 2021), 16, https://www.statedevelopment.qld.gov.au/industry/industry-support/qld-charter-for-local-content.

other industries, local can refer to the country of origin of goods, so "local" may mean anywhere inside that entire country.

Many local governments have much more geographical local buying policies, where businesses located within their own government areas are favoured. Local governments that have a local buying policy in place will often allocate a weighting to tenders received from *truly local* businesses. This can be quite substantial—I have seen weightings of up to 25%—so being a *truly local* business can be a real competitive advantage.

Most local buying or local content programs will have a pre-qualification or registration process. Mostly, they are pretty easy to navigate through, because the whole idea of them is to recruit smaller, local firms that don't have an entire procurement department to deal with lots of paperwork. Another advantage of local buying programs is that they often have better payment terms than the company's normal payment terms.

> **In the real world ...**
> *Resources and mining giant BHP Billiton subsidiary BHP Billiton Mitsubishi Alliance (BMA) runs a Local Buying Program. Only local businesses with less than 25 full-time equivalent employees which are physically located in the specified local government areas are eligible to participate in the program. There is a simplified pre-qualification process and a dedicated team to help small businesses use the program successfully. Payment terms under the local buying program are much more favourable to small business. In the first three years of operation, the average payment time was just 11 days as opposed to 60 days under normal contract arrangements. That figure is now down to seven days.*

The first place to look for a local content or preference arrangements is with your city, district or regional councils. Most of them will have information about the program on their website, including details about how to register. If you can't find anything there, make the phone call and find out if there is one, and if so, how you go about registering as a supplier.

Your next stop is to look at all the major companies that are operating in your vicinity. Include Tier 2 companies in your search (companies that will be supplying to Tier 1 companies), as they will often be a better target than the corporate giants, but you will still be supplying to a company larger than your own, and if you do a good job, good news travels up the supply chain. For each company, search their website to find out if they have a local buy or local content policy, and if they do, how you go about getting your company listed as a potential supplier.

Chapter 37
Go/No-Go Decisions

So, now you know where to find potential tenders and RFPs. But that doesn't mean that you should have a go at every single one you think sounds interesting. You need to be a bit strategic about this, and not chase every opportunity just because it's there.

Finding the right opportunities and then preparing tenders and proposals can be a very expensive exercise. Unless you subscribe to one of the commercial tender databases that will alert you to all possibilities in your realm of interest, somebody in your company will have to spend at least an hour every week scouring the internet looking for available tenders. Then comes the expensive part—researching, writing, costing, editing, and proofreading your submission.

Certainly, you could just copy and paste the last documents you prepared (and there are plenty of your big competitors who do exactly that), but in doing so, are you really addressing your prospect's individual problems and circumstances?

To have consistent success with your proposals and tenders, you have to put in a bit of effort, and that costs money.

How much money should you be spending on your tenders and proposals? There are many, many variables in this equation. If you are in a preferred supplier position, you may be simply asked to "email through a price". On the other hand, you may be asked to fill out one of those 630-row spreadsheets I mentioned before. However, an industry standard metric is that you should be spending 0.5% -2% of the profit available on the project the proposal is for.

You should look to spend between 0.5% and 2% of the profit available on a project in preparing your proposal.

So, you need to have some sort of a filter to choose the ones where you have the best chance of success, and that filter is a ***go/no-go decision checklist***. The go/no-go decision checklist asks you a series of questions that will help you to decide whether to commit resources to this particular opportunity or not.

Go/no-go checklists come in many forms, but all will lead you through the same general questions, such as:
- Are you the incumbent supplier? If not, do you know who is? Can you find out about the incumbent?
- Are you the only company that has been approached for this opportunity? If not, do you know who your competition is?
- Do you know this customer, and does this customer know you?

- Have you worked for this customer before? If so, do you have a good relationship with them?
- Is the work within your skill set? Is it a good match for your company's strengths?
- Do you have the resources available to complete the work—people, machinery, etc.? If you don't, can you get them easily?
- Do you have the correct qualifications required?
- Will you have to partner with another company to complete this work? If so, have you approached them and come to an agreement?
- Can you meet the delivery deadlines specified for the work?
- Will you have to borrow money to complete the work? If so, have you made arrangements with your bank?
- Are there any risks associated with the contract? (Make sure you consider reputational risks as well as business risks.)
- Have you reviewed the proposed contract for any unfair or unusual requirements?
- Can you get the proposal written, with everyone's input, in time to proofread and check it before you press the send button?

Of course this is not an exhaustive list by any means. There may be other issues specific to your industry that should be considered. But if you take this checklist, sit with your team, and work through the questions one by one, you will avoid being the over-energetic puppy, and only chase the contracts that you actually have a good chance at winning.

A sample go/no-go checklist that I have used for many years is available for download from the Small Company, Big Business website, so please use it to avoid wasting resources chasing unicorns that you have absolutely no chance of catching.

Chapter 38
Writing Tenders and Proposals

How to Make Sure Your Tender Doesn't Fall at the First Hurdle

In my experience, the procurement teams of many large organisations exist in a parallel universe somewhere, virtually un-contactable and untouchable by us mere mortals. Consequently, it can be extremely difficult to find out what it is that they look for when evaluating tender submissions.

Having worked with several procurement teams over the years, I have managed to accumulate a list of the most common failures that they see, and what we should be paying attention to. Some of these will seem very obvious, but procurement officers reliably inform me that they see all manner of things in tender submissions, not all of which are "best practice".

Lack of attention to some of these basic items will mean that your tender submission will most probably be discarded immediately, without receiving any consideration at all.

What Do Tender Evaluation Teams Look For?

So what do large companies look for when evaluating tender responses? And what can you do to make your tender submissions more likely to be a winner, and not fall at the first hurdle?

Look for what they want

Read the documents carefully to see if there is any evaluation criteria included. This will tell you how much weight they are putting on the different elements of the tender.

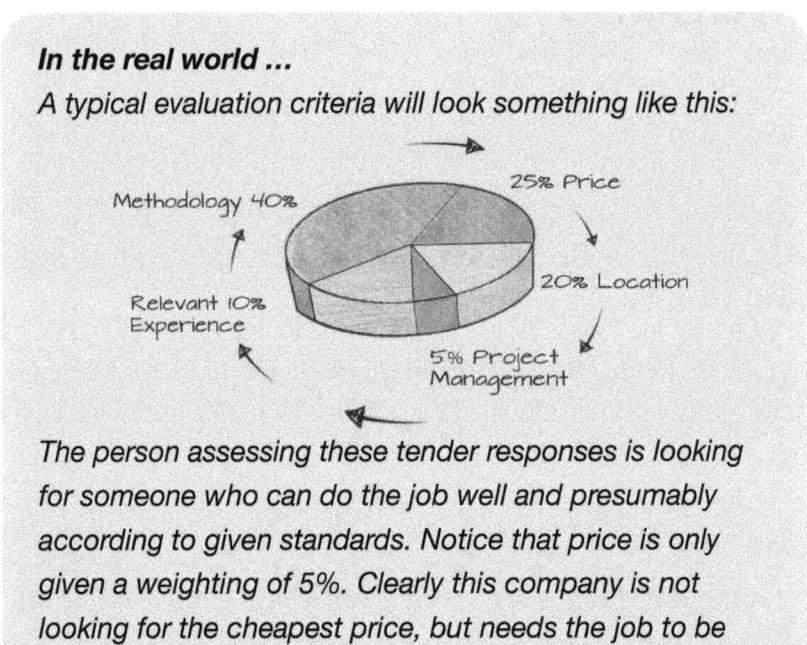

In the real world ...
A typical evaluation criteria will look something like this:

The person assessing these tender responses is looking for someone who can do the job well and presumably according to given standards. Notice that price is only given a weighting of 5%. Clearly this company is not looking for the cheapest price, but needs the job to be done extremely well.

Never assume anything

If you have a question about something in the tender, ask, and ask early. If anything is unclear, or you would just like some further clarification, pose the question as soon as possible. A tender can be lost due to a lack of clarity about something that is sometimes very straightforward.

Articulate the benefit
Make sure you are very clear on the benefit that your solution/product/service will provide for your prospective client. To help you get clear on this, complete a Value Proposition Canvas[32] before you start. A Value Proposition Canvas is a handy tool that will capture the essence of the value you provide to your clients on a single page.

Contact only the people specified
Each tender will have a designated contact; direct all questions or correspondence to them only. That way you can ensure that you are getting the correct and official answers to your questions.

Answer ALL the questions
Never, ever leave questions blank. The tender evaluation team do not know if you have overlooked it or simply ignored it. This is the fast-track way to have your tender submission discarded immediately.

Don't put N/A
If a question is not applicable to you, tell them why. A short sentence is sufficient so the tender evaluation team know that it really isn't applicable to you, not that you just think so.

Don't send them hunting for documents
By all means include attachments to help your business case but give at least a brief description of what those documents are within the tender, not just a note to "see attachment".

---

32 Alexander Osterwalder, Yves Pigneur, Greg Bernarda, and Alan Smith, 2014, *Value Proposition Design: How to Create Products and Services Customers Want* (New Jersey: John Wiley & Sons, 2014).

Always emphasise your strengths

Emphasise your strengths, not your competitor's weaknesses. Ensure that you emphasise how your strengths will assist your prospective client. Doing this will raise questions in your client's mind about whether your competitor can perform as well as you can.

If you need more time, ask early

If you really do need more time, make sure you put in a request early. If you ask the day before the deadline, you can be sure that your request will be denied.

If you aren't qualified, don't bid

Make sure you read the eligibility criteria and proposed contract carefully before you start writing. Many tenders will have minimum requirements for insurances, professional qualifications, contract conditions, etc. If you don't meet their criteria, your submission will be ruled out. (A possible exception here is where you submit a bid, even though you may not be fully qualified, just to get "on their radar". Make sure you have thought this through properly, though. You don't want to appear incompetent.)

Follow their format

If they have given you a form or spreadsheet to complete, use it. From experience, I know that some of these can be difficult to follow. However, they are usually trying to achieve a situation where they can compare apples with apples. Don't give them oranges. Granted, some of these spreadsheets may even verge on the ridiculous, but you have to follow the rules.

Use their language

Every industry has its own language and acronyms. Use their language and terminology to show that you really do understand them and their problem.

Showcase relevant experience

Include information on projects or work you have completed that would be comparable in size, value, and risk profile to the one you are tendering for. This will give the evaluation team insight into what you are capable of. Make them relevant though—something you did 20 years ago won't interest them.

Give them the full story

You are not sitting beside the tender evaluation team when they read your submission, so they can't ask questions to find out what you mean. Even if you've done work for that company for years, don't presume that they know you and what it is that you do. While you may have done work or provided services to that company for years, not all the members of the evaluation panel will know you. They may (and probably will) be located thousands of miles away, or even on another continent.

Even if you have done work for that company for years, don't presume that they know you, and what it is that you do.

Provide referees who will help your bid

Always provide referees for work and projects that you showcase in your tender. Be sure that they will provide a good reference for you, and let them know that you would like to provide their name as a referee. There would be nothing worse than having your prospective client call a referee and getting "I've never heard of them" in response.

Justify your non-conformances

If you propose a non-conforming tender, make sure you spell out the benefit of the non-conformance. Sometimes, with the best will in the world, the team preparing a tender get it wrong, or there may be a new and better way that you have devised to achieve the same outcome. If so, by all means propose the new or better way as a non-conforming tender. But make sure that you clearly identify the benefit.

Don't re-write War and Peace

Keep your answers succinct and to the point. It's ok to repeat information if it is relevant to more than one question (as opposed to "see question 7").

No jargon

If you are using abbreviations and acronyms, include a glossary. Not everyone on the tender evaluation team will be a technical specialist in your field, so give them the best chance of understanding what you are talking about.

Writing Isn't the End of the Tendering Task

Most of us think that getting the words down on paper and getting the pricing right are the most important parts of preparing proposal and tender documents for our prospective clients. We spend hours trying to second-guess what the competition will be offering and delving through management accounts to get the most accurate costings we can come up with (well, we should ...).

It's not just about the price. There are other important things to think about.

There are several aspects of your proposal documents that have a huge influence on whether your proposal gets noticed and read, or discarded in the first round.

Fonts

I hope by now I have convinced you that the pricing part of your client proposals is just the start. Winning contracts is a competitive business, and you need to give your proposals every possible chance to shine and stand above your competitors.

One of those aspects is the font you use. Believe it or not the font you use can have a significant impact on whether your proposal is even read, let alone read *properly*.

There is an entire body of research on fonts. Serif fonts—the ones with the extra little bits at the top and bottom of most of the letters (i.e., Times New Roman) are considered to be more readable on the paper page and have a more formal look, which is appropriate for your business proposals. Sans-serif fonts—where there are no extra bits (i.e., Ariel or Helvetica)—are considered to be better for use on screens and in digital documents.

Headings can be a bit more free-range. If you have a look at a post published on LinkedIn (preferably one of mine), you will notice that LinkedIn uses a serif font for the body of the posts, but a sans-serif font for the headings.

It is also ok to use some bold and italics to highlight particular key points you don't want skimmed over. But not too much, otherwise it loses its effectiveness.

Which serif fonts should you use?

The most commonly used serif fonts for proposal writing are Times New Roman and Georgia. However, the winner in the believability stakes is Baskerville.

The *New York Times* conducted some research in 2012[33] on which fonts were the most "believable". They found that the font

---

33 Morris, E., 2012, Hear, All Ye People; Hearken, O Earth (Part 1) https://archive.nytimes.com/opinionator.blogs.nytimes.com/2012/08/08/hear-all-ye-people-hearken-o-earth/, accessed 29 January 2023.

used actually did make a difference to whether their readers believed a series of statements.

Farfetched as it may seem, more people agreed with a statement when it was written in Baskerville. Taking it even further, the research showed that Baskerville was also the font that had the lowest "disagreement" score. After I read about this, I started using Baskerville in my own proposals and tenders. I certainly did increase my success rate, but that could just as easily be due to the fact that I was getting better and better at writing convincingly. Correlation is not causation, but I've kept using Baskerville—just in case.

Images and graphics

They say that a picture is worth a thousand words, and this is most certainly the case when your tender is being evaluated. No tender reader will ever read the entire script of every tender they receive, so using excellent images and graphics that help tell your story and answer their questions can really help. The human brain is attuned to notice and decode images. Remember how you learned to read? Your first reading books had lots of pictures and very few words. The pictures give clues to the meaning of the words.

But like anything good, moderation is the key, and images can be overdone or badly done. There are guidelines and tips on good—and bad—practice, but three important rules for using images in your documents are:

1. Only use images that lend value to your story. They should also have aesthetic value, but the most important attribute is that every image or graphic should be supporting your central theme.
2. Consider using graphs rather tables to express data. Graphs tell readers a story much quicker than if they have to try to interpret a series of figures.
3. Introduce each image or graphic in the text and give it a meaningful caption that adds to your story.

Example:

Grammar and spelling

Get someone who can spell and someone who is a grammar pedant to proofread your writing.

Do not omit this step.

Ever.

Following Up

Your proposal has now been written, reviewed, and sent off to your prospect. What happens next?

If you have replied to a tender, you should know exactly how long you have to wait for an answer, as this information would be contained in the tender documents. However, if you are replying to a request for proposal (RFP), you may not. Even some organisations that use tenders do not do their losing tenderers the courtesy of letting them know that someone else has been successful.

Whether you are successful or not, you should always follow up with your prospect for feedback on your proposal. Some large organisations will automatically give written or verbal feedback without you asking for it, but this is rarer than it should be.

When asking for feedback, be polite—being nasty because you didn't get the job won't do your future chances any good. I fully understand that you may feel hurt when you are not the chosen bidder, especially when the contract is significant enough to affect your business. But you must maintain your professionalism at all times and not give in to the temptation to yell "DO YOU KNOW HOW MUCH THIS TENDER COST ME TO PREPARE?" at the procurement officer. Some may be willing to share the scores that you received on the evaluation criteria, but most won't.

What you are trying to find out is what you can do better next time. What was it in your submission that could have been done better in order to have been successful? How did your submission compare to your competitors on price and value for money? Did your submission comply with all the requirements?

> **In the real world ...**
> *I too have had sessions of tears and felt like screaming at the procurement officer. At one point we lost a tender we fully expected to win as the incumbent, but also because of the nature and location of the work and the fact that we had gone above and beyond to get this particular client out of some deep doo-doo. However, price proved to be the overriding factor, and a competitor with untrained personnel and sub-standard equipment was granted the project. The size of the project, and the fact that we were the incumbent, meant that I had to let one of our team go who had been designated and trained for that project. That was an awful day—one of the worst in my 25-year business history.*

SECTION 7
SO YOU'VE WON THE CONTRACT— NOW WHAT?

Congratulations! You've done all the hard work, and finally received that precious email.

"Thank you for your fee proposal for the XXXX project.

On this occasion you have been successful. ABC Pty Ltd. looks forward to working with you on this project."

In our office, we have a cow bell. When one of these emails arrives, somebody rings the cowbell to let everyone know that we have another job to do. Hearing the cowbell usually means a five to ten minute time out while we discuss the new project, often over a cup of tea or coffee. To us, it is important to celebrate these wins as a team. Every person has contributed to the success of that proposal, whether they worked on it directly or not.

We also know that once the cow bell has been rung, the hard work really begins—delivering the project on time, on budget, to specification, with a happy customer.

Welcome to the world of project management.

Chapter 39
Introduction to Project Management

Once your small business starts to grow, you will be taking on bigger and bigger jobs. They will typically take longer and involve more people and resources than before. Congratulations! You are now at the stage of having to step up and be a ***project manager***.

Unfortunately, this is where many small business owners trip up, sometimes fatally. Like any business owner, you know that winning work is always a major challenge. Everyone has competition, and winning work takes a significant portion of your time.

Having done all the hard work to win a contract, though, many business owners and managers then fail to run the project well. An opportunity turns into a loss, or at least a smaller profit than there should have been. The customer gets cross and threatens to withdraw the contract.

How does this happen? How does such a golden opportunity turn sour? It is all in how the project is managed.

Project management is a formal discipline of study, like engineering. You can study for a certificate or diploma, right up to a master's degree or PhD. A simple Google search will give you hundreds of thousands of definitions of a project, but the one I like is this one from the Project Management Institute, an organisation for project management professionals:

> *"A project is a temporary endeavour undertaken to create a unique product, service or result."*[34]

The picture below shows a couple of kids involved in a project. It's a temporary endeavour—the day at the beach will end—the kids are undertaking to create a unique product—every sandcastle is certainly unique.

SANDCASTLES

Every project has three distinctive characteristics:
- a definite beginning and end
- a unique outcome
- it uses resources to create that unique outcome

---

34 Project Management Institute, publisher. (2021). The standard for project management and a guide to the project management body of knowledge. (Seventh edition.). Project Management Institute, Inc.

That sounds quite simple in theory, but we all know that things don't always work out the way they are supposed to in theory.

There's an old joke amongst project managers about the six phases of a project:[35]
1. Unbounded enthusiasm,
2. Total disillusionment,
3. Panic, hysteria and overtime,
4. Frantic search for the guilty,
5. Punishment of the innocent, and
6. Reward for the uninvolved.

To illustrate the point, here are some terrifying statistics that should convince you that project management is yet another business skill that you really have to master:[36]
- Only 30% of projects succeed. That is, they are on budget, on time, with the required outcome.
- 42% of companies don't understand the need or importance of project management.
- Using a project management process reduces the failure rate to 20% or below.
- 55% of project managers say that projects failed because of budget overruns.
- 60% of failed projects have a duration of less than one year.
- 77% of high performing companies understand the value of project management. Only 40% of low-performing companies understand the value of project management.
- The failure rate of projects with budgets over $1 million is 50% higher than the failure rate of projects with budgets below $350,000.

---

35 Different versions of this list appear in many business books, but the theme is consistent.
36 "Project Management Statistics: Trends and Common Mistakes in 2022," Teamstage, last accessed 15 November, 2022, https://teamstage.io/project-management-statistics.

Why Do So Many Projects Fail?

There are multiple lists on the internet that explain the reasons for most project failures, but this graphic seemed to capture the essence. Let's look at the three big project stumbling blocks.

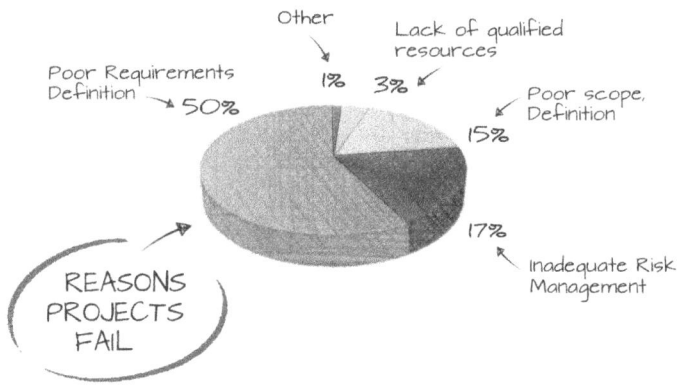

Source: ESI International survey of 2000 business professionals

Poor requirements definition—50%

I am sure that you have seen the cartoon below before. It's a beautiful illustration of what a poor requirements definition can produce.

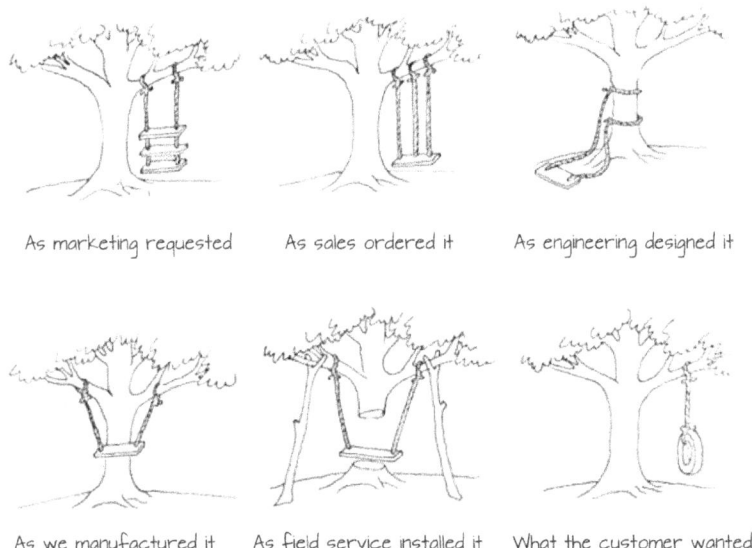

As the biggest single cause of project failure, it is obvious that this is where you should be spending significant time and effort. Many industries and professionals have developed questionnaires, interviews, or other means to capture an accurate and complete definition of exactly what the customer wants. What the customer really wants as that unique outcome I mentioned earlier needs to be detailed in laser-like detail.

Most web designers have a comprehensive questionnaire or design brief they require new clients to complete before they start building a new website. The questionnaire asks loads of questions about the business, what the site is supposed to achieve, who are the competitors, what features are needed, existing branding, etc. They will also usually ask you to nominate some other websites that you like and that you don't like, so they can zero in on what appeals to you. By doing this preparatory work, the web designer can be sure that both parties are very clear on what the new website should be. Your process for defining customer requirements should be similarly thorough.

Inadequate risk management—17%

Good project management means trying to foresee all the things that can go wrong with your project, or at least as many as you can at the outset of the project.

Risk management has five basic steps:
1. Identify all the things that could go wrong—the hazards.
2. Decide how likely it is that each of those things will go wrong.
3. If they do go wrong, what will the consequence be?
4. Think through what you can put in place to either prevent that risk from happening, or what you will do if that hazard does occur.
5. If something does go wrong, did your preparations work? If not, what do you need to do better next time?

All this information needs to be captured in writing and shared across your project team. Obviously, the risks facing your project won't stay the same over time, so you need to keep reviewing your initial risk assessment throughout the project. For example, imagine you had won a contract to build fences for an olive plantation back in 2007. At the time, investments in plantation companies such as this were tax deductible. Wealthy investors could reduce their tax burden by investing in olive groves, berry farms, and all sorts of other plantation-type schemes. As a good project manager, you would have assessed the risks associated with the project—such as rain delaying your progress—and hopefully put some plans in place to minimise any disruption. Then, suddenly, on February 5, 2007, the federal government announced that tax breaks for agricultural managed schemes were to be axed. Your contract, which you had probably already resourced, disappeared into thin air. Of course, the Covid-19 global pandemic which started in early 2020 taught us all about sudden changes. Whole industries, areas, and even countries were shut down with very little or zero warning. I have already mentioned how the companies. Now, we all have "Global Pandemic" in our risk management plans – or at least we should have.

For more comprehensive information on managing the risks that your business may face, treat yourself to a copy of my book Small Company, Big Crisis. How to prepare for, respond to, and recover from a business crisis. The book is available from my website bronwynreid.com.au, and all leading online bookstores.

> **In the real world ...**
> *One of the most spectacular project management failures in Australia is the project to put new pay and rostering software in the Queensland Department of Health. What started out in 2003 as a "whole of government" project to*
>
> >>

implement new HR and finance software morphed several times and through several suppliers, until it finally became a payroll system for Queensland Health. (Note the problem with requirements definition.) This project was awarded to IBM for $6.19 million. To cut a very long story short, the software that was eventually rolled out in 2010 didn't work, and thousands of employees were overpaid, underpaid, or not paid at all. One of my close friends is a nurse for Queensland Health, and is still receiving incorrect pay all these years later.

While it seems that at least one person had assessed the project risks—a department director tried to warn the minister of faults he had identified—the state government chose to not only ignore the project risk, but actually signed an agreement with IBM that it would not terminate the contract under any circumstances, and would relinquish all rights to take legal action for non-performance.

At last count, the system—which still isn't working—has cost Queensland taxpayers $1.25 billion. Yes, billion. In fact, just one of the inquiries into the debacle cost almost as much as the original project budget. The project is also widely acknowledged as one of the world's greatest IT project disasters.

Poor scope definition—15%

We have already looked at the problem of poor scope definition in Section 1, and how "scope creep" can kill your profit on a project.

A fuzzy scope at the beginning of a project is even more dangerous.

Consider my friend who wanted to build a new house. She

decided on a plan, house style, fittings, and all those other things you have to think about when you build a house. When the time came for the keys to be handed to her as the brand new owner, she told the builder that she wouldn't take possession because it wasn't finished. There was no driveway. The builder argued that a driveway was not part of the quote, and therefore not part of the scope. Who was right and who was wrong is not the issue here, but the problem would not have arisen with a more complete project scope.

The project scope gets right down to the nitty-gritty details of the work that has to be done and what has to be achieved, and then putting it in writing so that all the project stakeholders share the same understanding. You will need to think through the project goals, tasks, budget, timelines, deliverables, exclusions, assumptions, features, etc.

At the beginning of your work contract, make sure (at least as far as possible) you know exactly what your scope of works entails, what is expected, and make sure it is in writing.

In the real world ...
Our company had an experience where we accepted a contract to write a particular report, but our contribution formed a part of a much larger report. The report was a statutory requirement, so the company concerned had to complete and lodge it by a certain date. Our section of the report was duly lodged as a draft for review. The review by the senior environmental officer was interesting. He had assumed that our company was completing the entire report, and accordingly gave us a withering blast for doing a rubbish job. Gingerly, we had to point out that the scope of works that we had accepted very clearly spelt out what we were supposed to do.

There are many resources available online to help with this task, and I have included a simplified worksheet on the Small Company, Big Business website.

The Triple Constraints

As I said previously, this chapter is not intended to turn you into a fully-fledged project manager, but there is one aspect of project management theory and practice that you do need to understand—*the triple constraints*.

Every project is bounded by constraints on **time**, **cost**, and **scope** (what has to be done).

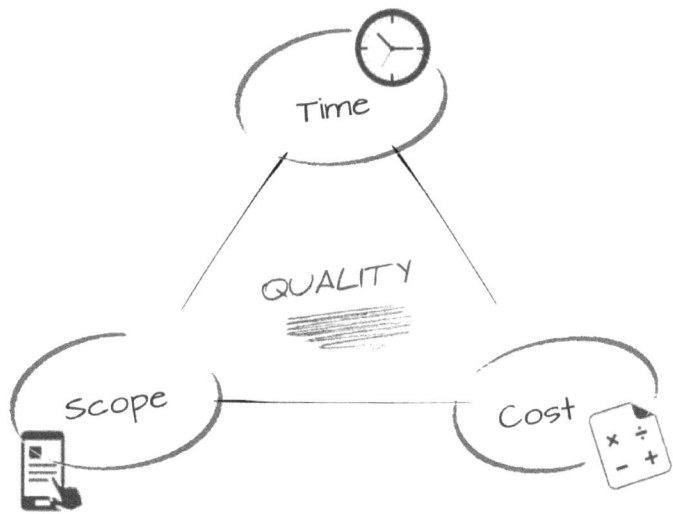

If you increase or decrease one of these elements and you still want a quality outcome, at least one of the others will have to change.

The resources boom in Australia from 2008 to 2012 was a textbook example of this. As the boom heated up, the rush was on to get all the coal out of the ground as soon as possible. Time was the constraint, so something had to give way. In this case, it was cost. Every problem was solved by throwing more money at it. The result was sky-high prices, for labour, equipment, real estate ...

Once the boom turned to bust, the dynamic changed, and cost became the constraint as the mining companies tried to rein in bloated expenses. Scope needed to be adjusted as project after project was shelved and maintenance activities were ratcheted back to bare minimum or below. I would argue that quality also gave way, as cheaper contractors replaced those who had provided good service during the boom.

So, for every project you undertake, you need to understand the critical drivers. Doing this simple exercise will go a long way towards exposing the potential threats and risks in your project. And there is a handy tool to help you do just that – the Priority Matrix. For each project, use the Matrix to think about what really matters. For Time, Cost and Scope, will you:

- Accept: Let this factor be as large as it needs to be to get the project done.
- Constrain: This factor has a limit, so you must pro-actively work to ensure that limit is met.
- Enhance: This factor needs to be as large as possible, so you must work pro-actively to increase it.

In the real world

Imagine that you are a website designer. On Friday morning, a client approaches you to build their new website. But there's a catch. They need it live for their product launch next Wednesday. What to do?

Time is a constraint, so Cost or Quality will have to be compromised.

Quality. We could build a single page website that will get them through the launch and build the rest later.

Cost: Bring the entire creative team in for the weekend and pay them overtime.

PRIORITY MATRIX	Accept	Constrain	Enhance
Time		✓	
Cost	✓		
Scope	✓		

Project Budgets

I know project budgets are arguably an alternative form of fiction writing, but you must prepare one nonetheless. If you have nothing to guide you (and your team, and your client) you will definitely blow out your costs.

If you have your management accounting under control (remember we looked at that in Section 3?), you will know exactly what all the elements of your project will cost you and you will be able to build up your budget from there, piece by piece. Once you have done your first few project budgets, it will become much easier for you, and you will probably develop your own template that will allow you to quickly fill in the blanks for ensuing projects. Not only will the budgeting process become easier, but you will be able to look back on your previous projects to see how far out your estimates were, and keep improving your skill.

Just like your risk analysis, you will have to re-visit your budget constantly throughout the project. Transparency is vital in your budget reviews and updates, from everyone involved in the project. You don't want to get to the end and find a cost blow-out surprise.

> *In the real world ...*
> *Several years ago, our consultancy company worked on a research report under extreme time pressure.*
>
> >>

We estimated the number of hours it would take us to complete the report, and that estimate was used in the project budget. Because it was a new and unknown topic, we had to be very careful not to let the project time blow out. As there were four of us working simultaneously on the report, we used our time management software to calculate time versus budget on a daily and, towards the end of the project, two-hourly basis to make sure we were on track.

Chapter 40
Keep Your Customer Close

Apart from managing your project well in terms of the scope, risk management, budgeting, etc., the other big secret to ongoing project success is keeping in touch with your customer. There has probably been at least one time in your life when a significant other has ended a relationship because you simply weren't paying them enough attention. Clients are just the same.

In fact, one of your most important tasks as a small business owner serving a big company is to form a close and trusting relationship with your company contact, and keep them informed—always. Your role is to make them look good to the people further up the ladder, so they must know that they can call on you for advice and assistance—even after hours if really necessary—to get them out of a pickle. In return, you will be their first port of call when new work comes up, and you'll have the incumbent's advantage.

> *60% of incumbents win tenders, so the odds are certainly in your favour.*

And it's not just your immediate contact that you should be wooing. Identify who else within the organisation is impacted by your product or service. Is there another person within the same department? Someone further up or down the chain of command perhaps?

This person (or people) should also be the target of your affection and attention. Let them know what you and your company do, how you fit in, and the value you provide. Include them in emails and, if possible, invite them into meetings. If you have sales collateral, such as slide presentations and brochures, make sure that they have them all, and the latest versions.

People further up the chain of command are particularly useful to have in your circle of influence. There is a large probability that the person further up the pecking order has influence over purchasing decisions. This is particularly valuable when budgets are restricted, as happens in periods of economic downturn. The first reaction of large organisations in times like this is to cut spending, and move spending authority up a couple of tiers. We have seen employees who previously had authority to spend up to $40,000 have their spending authority cut to just a few hundred dollars. One immediate effect of this is that decisions just don't get made at all. If the person that is now in charge of purchasing your products and services is already familiar with your company, you will be in a much better position to retain your status as a reliable supplier.

> *You never know when additional people you're working with might move position, company, or form relationships of value to you with others.*

It is also always good to be aware of how your target customer's reward system works. In companies and industries where people move around and change jobs frequently, how their key performance indicators (KPIs) are structured and how they are rewarded can be vital information. The most obvious KPI is the eternal one of cost-cutting. If your contact is being rewarded for cutting costs, and this is their number one KPI, you could be in real difficulty. Cutting costs by accepting lower standards or narrowing the amount of work to be done will make that person look like a hero—for the short term. But if they will be moving on and won't be around to reap the consequences of accepting lower quality, there will be an enormous temptation for them to take the immediate reward offered by being a star cost-cutter.

In a large organisation with thousands or even hundreds of thousands of employees, you have to expect that your carefully-cultivated contact will eventually move on. There is no way to avoid this, especially if you have done your job of making your contact look good. Your contact will be destined for bigger and better things. If you've done your groundwork well and cultivated a wider circle of influence, this doesn't have to be a fatal blow, but merely a speed-bump along the path of your ongoing relationship with the company.

Of course, the upside of your valuable contact moving on is that they will take their goodwill towards you and your company with them to their new position or even to a new organisation. Over our years in business, by far the majority of the work that our consultancy firm has won has come through word-of-mouth referrals from people we have previously worked with. In that profession, people tend to move around a lot, both within a given company and from company to company, so relationships are critically important. But this can also be a double edged sword. If you have a bad relationship with someone for whatever reason (either warranted or unwarranted), it can be very damaging to your prospects and potential to win work.

The important lesson is to keep your contacts close. If they begin to take you for granted, your relationship is likely to cool off. Your job is to constantly remind them of the value you provide, and how you help them to achieve their own objectives—both personal and corporate. And it's not solely about keeping relationships alive. Research shows that two-thirds of buyers of professional services don't know all the services that their suppliers can offer, but just over half of them are interested in finding out about additional services.[37] That equates to a lot of money being left on the table by suppliers that could easily be captured by simply maintaining good communications and relationships.

---

37   Hinge Research Institute, *How Buyers Buy*, 2013, https://hingemarketing.com/library/article/how_buyers_buy_professional_services_buyers_study.

Chapter 41
Putting it All Together

Now that you've made it to the end of this book, the first thing I wish to say to you is thanks. Thank you for paying me the compliment of staying with me to the end. I know how precious time is to any small business owner, so I trust you found something that either inspires or educates you in what I have written. As I said in the Introduction, this book is based on my own years of experience, as well as countless conversations with other small business owners in the same boat. My hope is that by sharing my experiences, I have helped you to drastically reduce the time and cost it takes you to get your *small business ready to do big* business and maybe even start punching well above your weight in your industry.

Just Get Started

The next thing I would like to say to you is—just get started. You made it past Section 2, so you have obviously made the commitment to grow out of the Struggle Zone. Now you have to do it, and this is where many small business owners struggle. I have seen countless SME operators attend workshops and courses to learn and improve their skills. They leave the venue armed with their workbook and a ton of good intentions, and then do nothing. Getting your company ready to successfully land big customers is a lot of work, and only full commitment will suffice.

I implore you to not waste the investment you have made in reading this book. Put your new-found knowledge to work to get your business buzzing. I acknowledge that it's not easy, but I've mapped out the steps for you to follow.

Let's Reflect on This Journey So Far

There are five key things I hope you'll have embraced from reading this book. So let's look back at those. You will now be well on your way to thinking bigger and better about these points.

Understanding your buyer—you've learned how big organisations think. Understand that your target customer is very, very different to you and the customers you have been serving up until now. You are going to have to change the way you operate your business, as well as your mindset.

Set your foundations—you know what essentials need to be in place. It's impossible to build a growing business on wobbly foundations, and big buyers need the assurance that their suppliers are stable and able to meet their requirements.

Simplify the complexity—you know how to get your business systems prioritised and sorted. Your big customers like to have a consistent product or service, delivered on time, every time. Robust, documented business systems are the only way to achieve this quality level.

You're able to make yourself known—you're ready to create a credible digital footprint. The world has changed for small business. An ad in the Yellow Pages or a local guide just isn't enough any longer. You need to have a website, a social media presence, and a business email at the minimum. And the social media scene is constantly changing, so putting your digital strategy in place then leaving it alone is not an option.

You know how and why to tell your story—where the best opportunities are to shine like a diamond as you pitch for bigger business. The days of a handshake deal over a coffee are over when you enter the realm of big company contracts. Well-written proposals and tenders that tell your company's individual story and demonstrate the value you bring are required.

What's Next?

Start simple and start slow. Don't overwhelm yourself by thinking that you have to do everything at once. One step at a time—in the order I have laid them out in this book—is the secret to success.

Don't be afraid to ask for help. Many of these steps to supplier success will require the input of specialist providers and I have already pointed out the potential downside of cost saving when it comes to hiring lawyers, accountants, and other professionals. By the way, this is another excellent reason to take things one step at a time—trying to do everything at once would cost you a pretty penny and leave you with no cash in your business. I have spent countless hours researching and learning the required skills as we have dealt with bigger and bigger companies, but I also know when to call in the experts. For example, there's no way I would even contemplate building a website or completing tax returns myself. Be prepared to pay and hire the right people at the right time.

If you would like to have me in your corner as you navigate the sometimes-treacherous waters of small business, go to the (page 280) and contact me via the details listed there.

- **Don't start pitching until you are ready.** You may only get one chance to land your dream client. Make sure you really understand them and have what they need before you begin your pitch. It may have taken years to get your first appointment. Your chances of getting a second appointment are still somewhere close to zero, so don't blow it by being unprepared.

My final piece of advice to you as you set off in search of your first big contract is …

- **Never forget the clients that helped you get to where you are now.** While having your new, bright, shiny big customer is wonderful, don't forget who supported you when your business was just a toddler with training wheels. Your new customer can be extremely demanding of your time, but dropping your existing clients is an extremely risky strategy.
- As my colleague Matthew Dunstan says, *"With a big deal, it's important to remember your 'bread and butter' revenue lines and not neglect them."*
- **And of course …** do what you do with pride. Your new big client has chosen you because you are the best person to solve their problem. Do good work. Be ethical! Bring your small business personal touch to your big business transactions. That's something that your big competitors simply cannot provide.

ACKNOWLEDGEMENTS

The first edition of this book took me significantly longer to finish than I would have liked or expected, but it did eventually get done. For that, I have several people to thank.

To my husband Ian Rankine. There is absolutely, positively, no way on earth that I would have come to this point without your love, help and support over the many years of our business and life partnership.

Our two wonderful children, Sala and Sam. I know that you didn't suffer from over-mothering as your father and I combined our parenting duties with starting and growing our businesses. You have both developed into beautiful adults, and I know you will both make your mark in the world by doing good things. Thank you for believing in me and being my support system when I needed one.

There are many, many people who were involved in the creation of this book. Bev Ryan started me on this author's journey when I won the Queensland Rural, Regional and Remote Women's Network Strong Women Leadership Award for Business back in 2013.

Dixie Carlton has been my taskmaster and mentor in making this second edition appear. I can't thank Dixie enough for persisting with me in getting this finished.

My designers, the team at BrandStrong and Cheryl Tompkins

at CADesignIT. Ann Dettori and her team at Independent Ink who made the whole thing happen and helped me though the printing and publishing maze.

Andrew Griffiths, my guru and mentor on the first edition has continued to be provide me with endless support, wisdom, friendship and humour.

To the team at 4T Consultants, both past and present, thank you for stepping in and allowing me to take the time needed to complete it. In particular, thank you Kelle for bearing the brunt of my work as this book neared completion. 4T is what it is due to your collective efforts. As Claire said at one Friday drinks on the verandah, "4T isn't a job, it's a lifestyle!"

About the Author

Bronwyn Reid is a specialist in navigating the gap between large companies and small businesses who want to do better business with each other. Her expertise is transformative when it comes to fully understanding and translating the sometimes complex and disparate language each uses. It is that language difference that often prevents the clear communication necessary for win-win business partnerships and alliances.

Bronwyn is particularly focused on regional and rural business, supply chain management, and building sustainable companies.

- Acclaimed Boom and Bust Business Specialist
- Successful founder of two award-winning businesses in regional Queensland
- Named as an international Stevie Award Winner 2022 for Thought Leadership
- Multi-award winning author of Small Company, Big Business and Small Company Big Crisis
- University lecturer for 12 years (part time) on business

She is best known for her strong business and community engagement roles in regional Queensland as a speaker, mentor, and collaborator.

Bronwyn's businesses have been supplying to national and international companies and all levels of government for over 26 years. She has brought all her experience of attracting, winning, and retaining work with these large organisations together in the Small Company, Big Business program, and in 2023 launches her Business Boosting Programs for Medium and Large organisations. This Program focuses on helping other SME's to secure and maintain contracts with large organisations.

For more on Bronwyn's availability as a speaker, strategist, and trainer, please visit:

www.bronwynreid.com.au

Further Information and Resources

The Small Company, Big Business Programs

The Small Company, Big Business Programs bring together Bronwyn's years of experience of dealing with big buyers and their supply chains. The program takes the business owner through the steps necessary for being a successful, reliable and profitable supplier to these big organisations.

There are also other places where you can find more of my content:

- Follow me on LinkedIn, Facebook, or join one of my audiences
- Book me to speak at your next event or present a workshop
- Read my other books

To find details on these options, go to:

www.smallcompanybigbusiness.com, or
BronwynReid.com.au/actionpage.

But wait, there's more ...

Welcome to the engine room of this book. You have reached the end. Congratulations! Hopefully you are thinking, "Wow, I got a lot out of this book", but you may also be feeling a little overwhelmed, and highly intoxicated with inspiration about what to do next to maximise your ability to do much bigger and better business with larger companies. Or, you may have skipped to the end, because I mentioned these added resources a couple of times throughout the book … Hopefully you'll go back and read the juicy bits you didn't get to yet. ☺

Either way – you're here now because you want more. And I'm going to give you so much more than you might have imagined possible. MY mission is to help as many small business owners and managers as I can, to get greater satisfaction, results, and thrills from putting all this into practice. So, I have a range of opportunities for you right now.

There are four options you can grab right now to get you fully focused and moving forward:

1) Come and hang out in my regular FREE Business Booster sessions.
2) Take one of my QUIZZES to see how far along the path you already are, and identify your priorities so you can start some planning and goal setting.
3) Download some of the many resources I offer to my database. Every month there's a new opportunity to grab hundreds of dollars worth of FREE STUFF.
4) Book an Unpack and Prioritise (UP) Session with me.

See the details for this on the next page.

Book an UP Session – Unpack & Prioritise

Working at a higher level of business and becoming part of a bigger supply chain is a big step. There's a chance you really do have it all together, BUT are feeling a bit overwhelmed – needing some guidance, a few strategies in place, and to map out your next steps. That's what I'm here for.

Taking advantage of greater opportunities in your business means knowing how to measure up in the eyes of those you wish to do bigger business with. There are some handy 'tricks' to that and I'm here to guide you through it. You will almost certainly benefit hugely from my mentoring or intensive sessions, and especially some of my training programs. But the very first step is to Unpack everything and then Prioritise things.

Here's a bit about how this works:

The UP (Unpack and Prioritise) Session is designed to help you identify your biggest challenges in relation to doing business with larger companies. By the end of it, my aim for you is to have some specific actions to take, within identified timelines, and know exactly what you need to prioritise as your next steps.

In our 90 minute UP Session I'll focus on helping you:

- Unpack your biggest opportunities;
- Identify the challenges to your maximising those opportunities;
- Work out what your best plan is to move forward – your Business Map if you like.

I'll also help you to identify:
- Any additional training, coaching, or development needs;
- Where your lowest hanging fruit really are;
- Where your risk exposures may lie, and what to do about that;

- Exactly what you need to do to be extremely attractive to big business.

So, let's do that!

Here's the details and booking options for the UP Sessions: www.bronwynreid.com.au/UPsessions

Ordering Additional Copies of this Book

If you have enjoyed this book, or know someone who would benefit from reading it, further copies are available at:

https://bronwynreid.com.au
Special rates are available for bulk orders.

www.ingramcontent.com/pod-product-compliance
Lightning Source LLC
Chambersburg PA
CBHW062031290426
44109CB00026B/2597